Portrait Drawing
for Kids

PORTRAIT DRAWING

for kids

A Step-By-Step Guide to Drawing Faces

Angela Rizza

ROCKRIDGE PRESS

Interior and Cover Designer: Eric Pratt
Photo Art Director/Art Manager: Tom Hood
Editor: Natasha Yglesias
Production Editor: Ashley Polikoff
Illustrations: Angela Rizza

ISBN: Print 978-1-64152-725-5 | eBook 978-1-64152-927-3

R0

Dedicated to my grandparents John and Martha Leone, who started me on my art journey, and to my parents for supporting me through it.

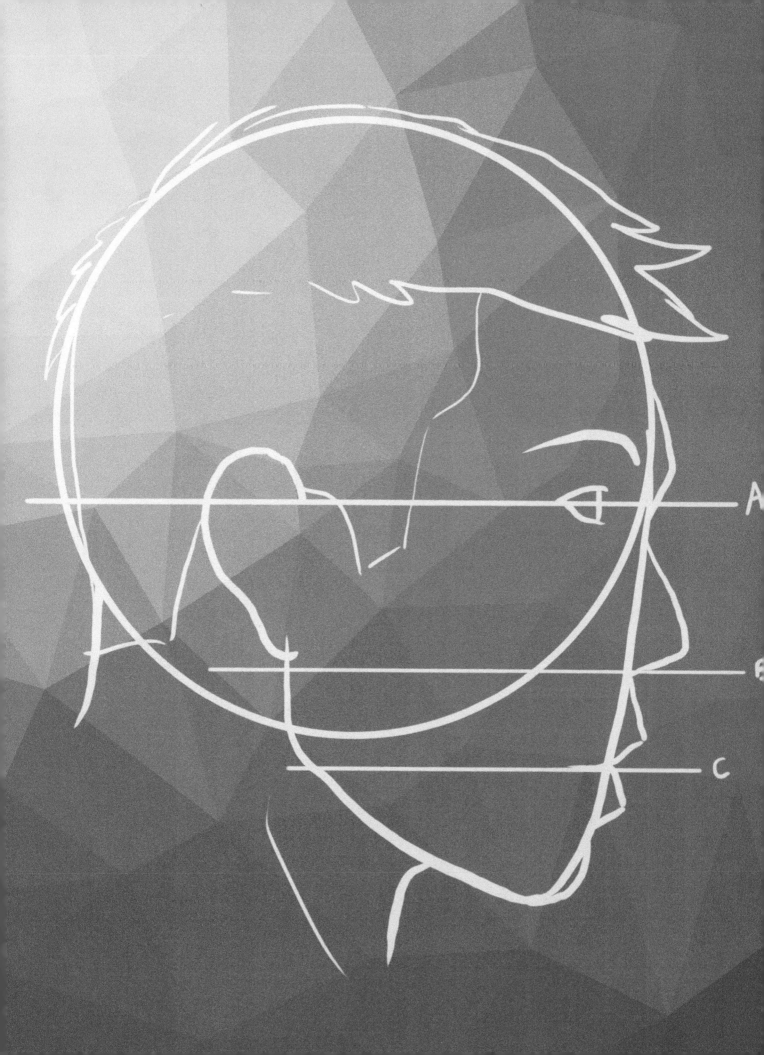

CONTENTS

INTRODUCTION

Hello, budding artists! Guess what: The selfie isn't just a modern-day thing! Through-out history, people have wanted portraits of themselves. In ancient civilizations, kings had their likenesses carved into statues and painted onto walls for all to see. Throughout the Renaissance, the wealthy had their portraits painted and hung in their homes as status symbols. And for hundreds of years, artists have been sitting in front of mirrors, capturing their reflections.

A selfie is a moment in time captured. It's a way to catch a memory of someone and keep it forever. A selfie can communicate who a person is, wordlessly. As an artist, you can draw how you or your friends want the world to see you and your story. No one is alike, so let's use this book to celebrate our uniqueness. By being open to our diverse world and observing its humanity, we elevate our art.

It can be easy to feel overwhelmed by illustrations in books and think you can't draw anything similar. I don't want you feeling that way, so I've broken down the drawings in this book into simple steps. And don't worry, nothing you draw has to be perfect. Your first few drawings may not look exactly as you intended, but remember that nobody learns without making mistakes, trying new things, and leaping out of their comfort zone.

Go at your own pace. If you feel like redoing an activity before moving on to the next, that's totally fine. Drawing should feel like fun, not like work.

Ready? Let's go!

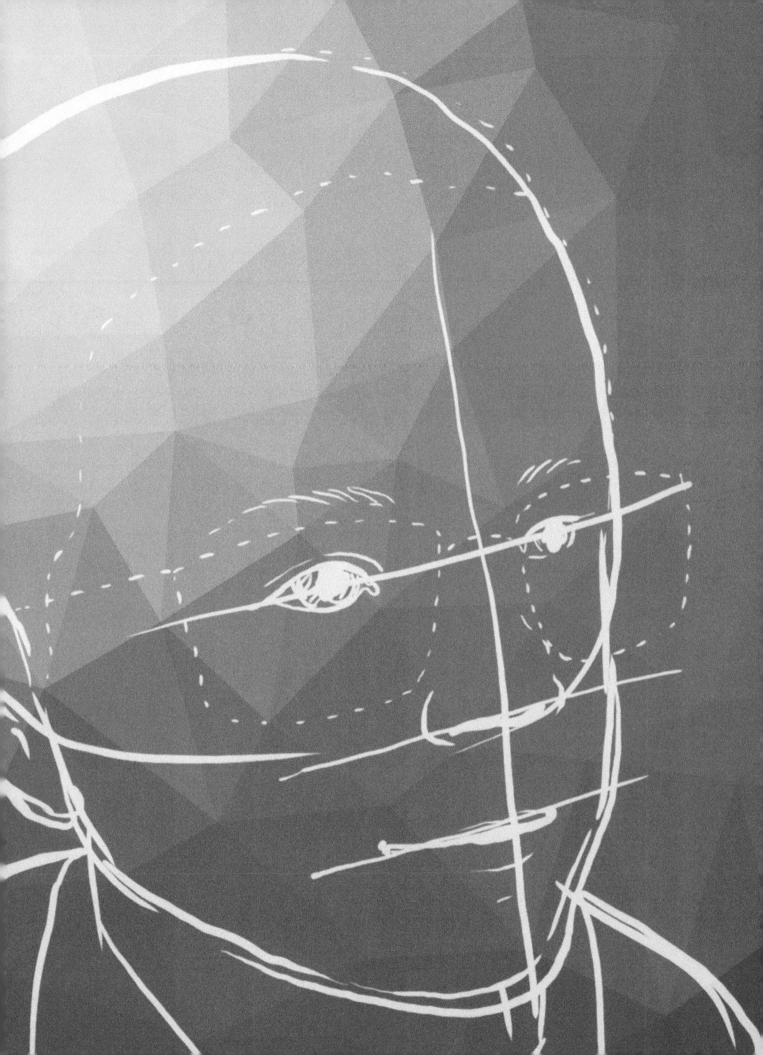

FOR TEACHERS AND PARENTS

In my previous book, *Figure Drawing for Kids*, space constraints meant I couldn't include everything I wanted to say about drawing faces. In this book, I'm able to expand that lesson. I discuss drawing portraits young and old, facial features, expressions, subject posing, and self-portraits. Kids can use lessons from my previous book—such as the portrait chapter—as a foundation, then go into detail with this book. This is my second how-to book and is based on the past decade of working as an illustrator and private teacher. I include foundation lessons I learned while getting my BFA at the Fashion Institute of Technology in New York City, as well as lessons I've developed through teaching art to elementary and middle school children.

In this book, I break down facial structures. I give a brief lesson in drawing basic foundational forms, and then provide step-by-step activities that touch on drawing more than just generic shapes. Faces are unique, and I hope to challenge young artists to draw what they see rather than to simply follow traditional formulas. The key to drawing a successful portrait is to capture someone's likeness, and to do that, we need to move beyond drawing an oval for an eye or a circle for a head.

I use a variety of subjects because the world is filled with an array of people and styles. I want to capture the likenesses of people you might see every day on the street, and not the academic or idealized depictions found in most books or magazines.

The goal of this book isn't to teach kids to copy images, but rather to get them to learn from the lessons and apply them to their future illustrations. The goal is to teach kids to look at and celebrate, through their creativity, what makes people different from each other. After following along with the lessons and activities, kids can take their newly attained knowledge and expand on it to create their own comics, graphic novels, paintings, drawings, and beyond.

HOW TO USE THIS BOOK

The first part of this book looks at each facial feature (eyes, nose, and mouth) individually, so you can learn how to draw them one at a time. The second part combines the features and discusses details beyond the face, like hair, clothing and accessories, coloring, composition, and shading.

Each activity starts with a short lesson and step-by-step drawings to show you the process and help you learn by seeing examples. Think of these drawings as guided practice; you will have your own drawing style and shouldn't feel any pressure to make exact copies of my drawings.

I start with lessons you can draw along with, but in the final chapters, I want you to go out and draw from life. You might ask a friend or family member to pose for their portrait, and I tell you how to gather your own ideas and references for your art.

You don't have to follow the lessons in any particular order. For example, if you're having trouble drawing a specific part of the face, you can always flip to a different lesson. Remember, practice makes perfect; repeating activities can help you improve your skills.

And feel free to try out your own ideas. Most of all, have fun!

TOOLS

You only need basic tools and materials for the lessons in the first half of this book. They are affordable and easily available. In later chapters, some activities include materials for color and shading, but there's no need to run out and buy a bunch of stuff—I sure didn't. Just use what you have on hand or what you're comfortable with.

Essentials

- Erasers

- Pencils (any type is fine)

- Sketchpad or sketchbook (labeled "mixed media"). A good size is 8.5 by 11 inches.

Nice to Have

- Acrylic paint (if you wish to paint in chapter 11)

- Colored pencils: Prismacolor pencils are great

- Colored markers

- Ink pens or markers, such as Micron or Sharpie (fine point)

- Pastels: chalk or oil

- Watercolor palette and brushes: You don't need lots of different colors, because you can make them all with the primary colors—red, yellow, and blue.

Part One

THE BASICS

Framing the Face

Heads can be round, oval, square, long, or short. Their features (eyes, nose, and mouth) can be just as varied.

Square   Round   Angular   Long   Oval   Rectangle

First, I draw a circle for the skull. Then I add a triangle for the lower jaw. Near the center of the circle, I draw three horizonal lines (*A*, *B*, and *C*). *A* has the pupils of the eyes, *B* the nose, and *C* the lips. The ears lie between *A* and *C*. These lines can be equally spaced, or you can change their **proportion** to create different personalities. Then I make a vertical line (*D*), which divides the face from the forehead through the nose to the chin.

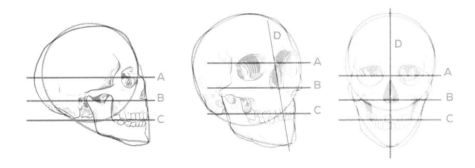

You can also tilt the sketch to show the face at different angles. So, although portraits may seem hard at first, it really comes down to drawing three lines and placing a few shapes on those lines.

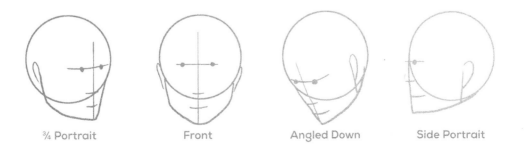

¾ Portrait   Front   Angled Down   Side Portrait

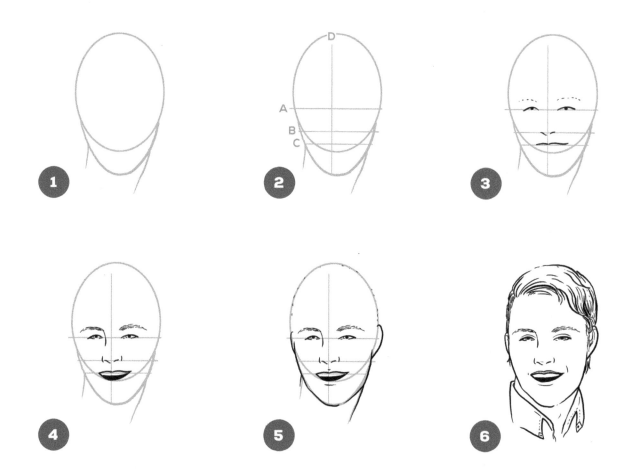

1 This subject has a long, narrow face, so lightly pencil an oval shape. Add a curvy triangle for the jaw and chin and a hint of neck.

2 Now add the *ABCD* lines. Let's give your subject a long nose and a big smile.

3 With a marker or darker pencil, draw the upper lip on line *C*, the nostrils on line *B*, and the pupils on line *A*. Draw the upper eyelids above line *A* and add a few dots where the eyebrows will be.

4 Define the eyes, nose, and mouth.

5 Now draw the face shape. Angle the lines to make the chin. For the hair, draw dashes to show how high it'll go. Draw the ears between lines *A* and *C*.

6 Add final details such as hair, lips, eyelids, and anything more.

Now that we've tried one together, practice a few on your own. Remember, your figures don't need to be perfect. Have fun!

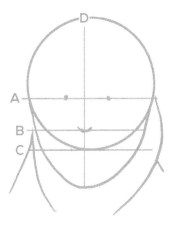

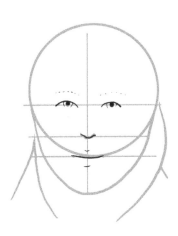

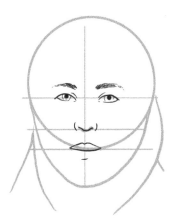

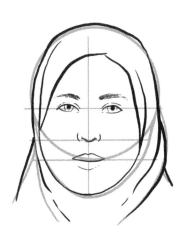

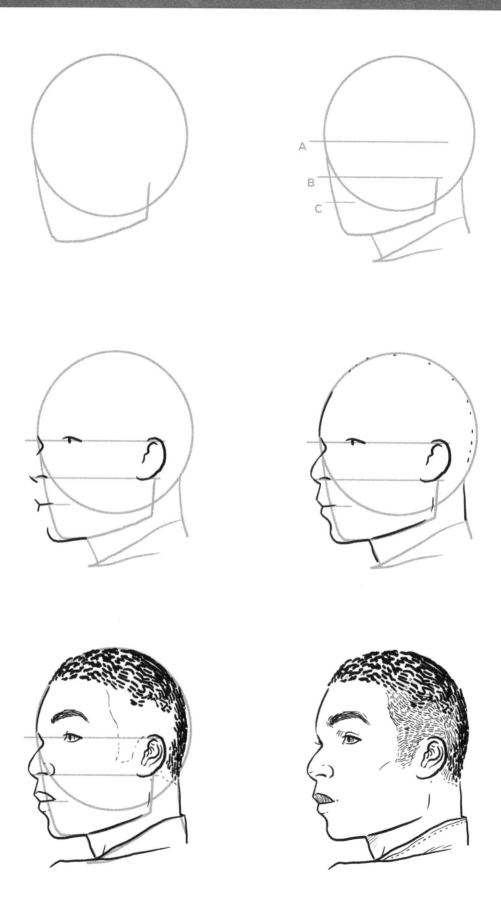

Eyes and Eyebrows

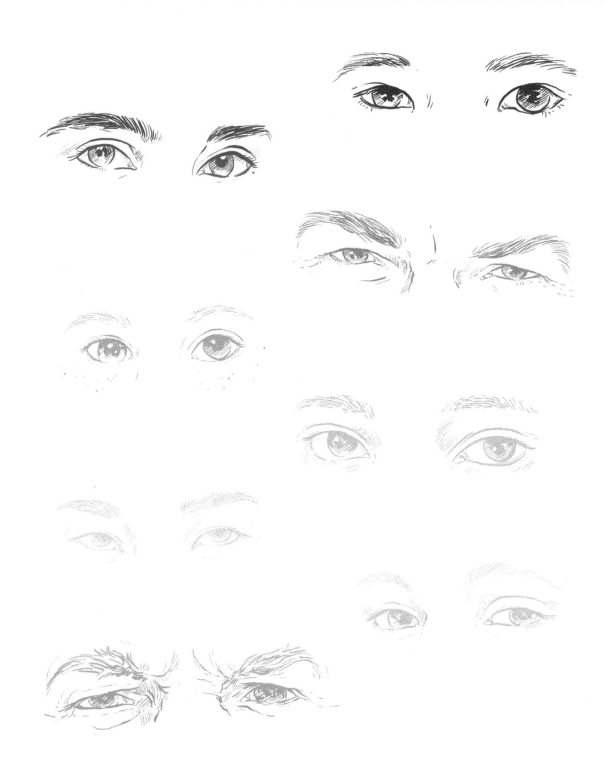

Eyes sit deeper in the face and capture more shadows than eyelids, which attract more light. The upper lid line is thick because of the eyelashes, but you don't have to draw every lash—a few curling around the edge of the eye is enough.

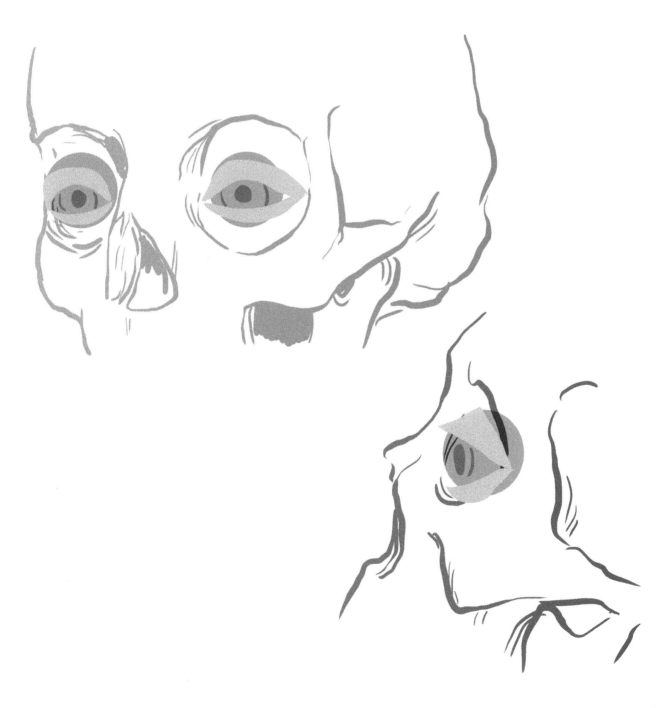

Eyeballs are reflective, so I use a black scribble for the pupil. I also shade the iris, making it darker around the upper lid, which adds **depth**. Unless the eyes are wide open, the top and bottom of the iris circle are usually cut off by the eyelids.

FRONT

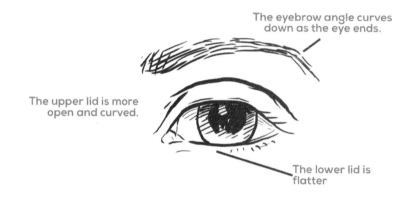

The eyebrow angle curves down as the eye ends.

The upper lid is more open and curved.

The lower lid is flatter

¾ VIEW

The eye closest to you is larger, and its shape is more almond.

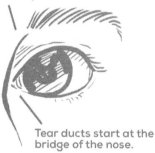

The eye that's further into the head turn is distorted. It appears as more round in shape.

Tear ducts start at the bridge of the nose.

SIDE

The iris is round, the lid makes a ❯ shape, and the lower lid is more curved.

Eyebrows start above the inner corner of the eye, then arch into a curve that peaks around the outer eye area. They then slope downward and usually end just past the length of the eye. I draw the hairs with some vertical lines in the center that slant toward the side of the head. A few randomly angled lines make brows look more natural.

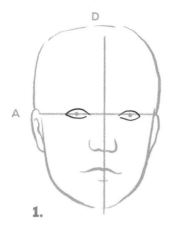

1.

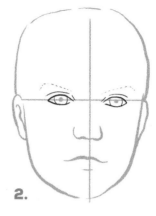

2.

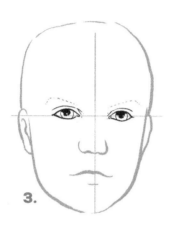

3.

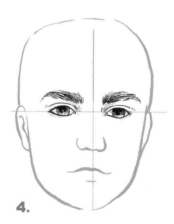

4.

1 Lightly sketch a basic head with a line for the mouth and a U shape for the nose. Draw the *D* line, then the *A* line. Draw an almond eye shape using a darker pencil. (Quick tip: The space between the eyes is usually the size of one eye.)

2 Draw the upper eyelid, following the shape of the eye. Then draw the iris. Dot where the eyebrows will go.

3 Add details. Draw a small, thin curve for the rim of the eyelids. The tear duct is oval. The upper eyelid isn't always a perfect curve, so add another fold of skin. Draw the pupil. Extend the upper corner line of the eyelid and make it thicker.

4 Using thin lines, shade the iris, dark to light, and some of the white of the eye (it's darker on the top of the eye). Add eyelashes and eyebrows. Shade a bit around the eye. Most shadows hit the area between the tear ducts and eyebrow and around the outside of the upper lid and side of the nose.

Now that we've tried one together, practice a few on your own. Remember, your figures don't need to be perfect. Have fun!

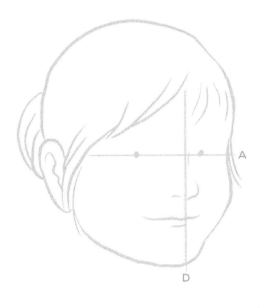

Nose and Mouth

The nose rests on the *D* line, dividing the center of the face. The nostril sides are often in line with where the eyebrows begin, and the outer corners are in line with the tear ducts. The nose is like a cone, narrowest right under the eyebrows and widening into a ball shape near the lips.

A mouth's upper lip is often shaped like two hills close together, while the lower lip is like an orange slice. Light hits the lips differently, so the upper lip is darker. In a resting face, lip length is usually the same distance as from one eye pupil to the other.

Keep in mind that too many details around the mouth can make a person look older. Also, you don't have to draw every tooth; instead, focus on the contrast between tooth color and the darkness inside the mouth. Include any detail like a missing tooth or gap.

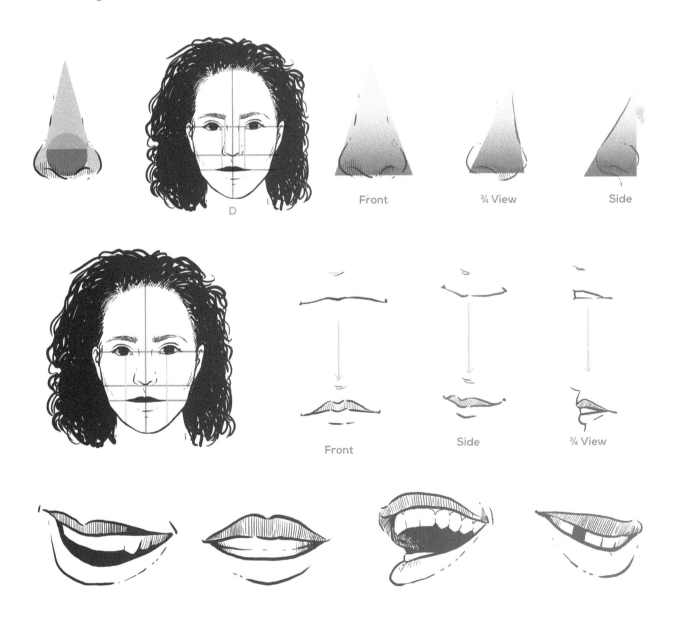

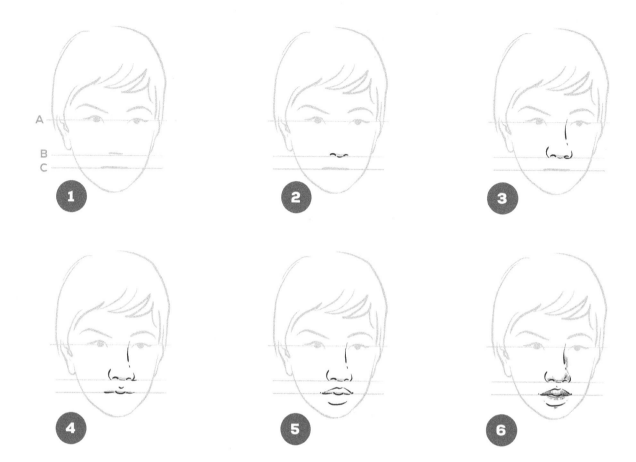

1   Draw a light sketch of a head with lines showing where the nose and mouth will be.

2   Draw the nostrils and nose tip.

3   Draw the bridge and side of the nose, making a broken line on the side of the face that will be in shadow. This line starts near the eyebrow and curves to the nostril.

4   On the C line, draw a line like a stretched-out M. Next, draw a little U shape in the center of the upper lip.

5   Use lines to connect the U to the corners of the mouth. For the lower lip, draw a simple, light stroke.

6   Often, less is more when drawing faces. Draw some delicate lines to show the curve of the nose and lips, and add shading to the dark side of the nose.

Now that we've tried one together, practice a few on your own. Remember, your figures don't need to be perfect. Have fun!

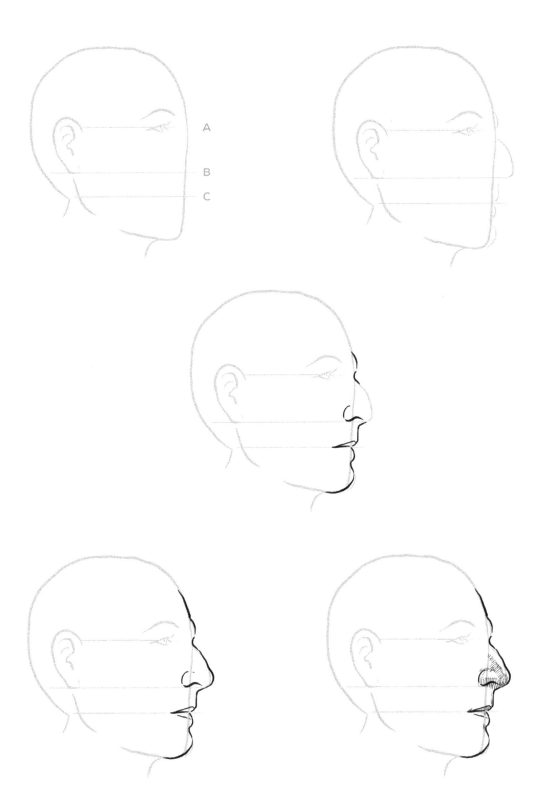

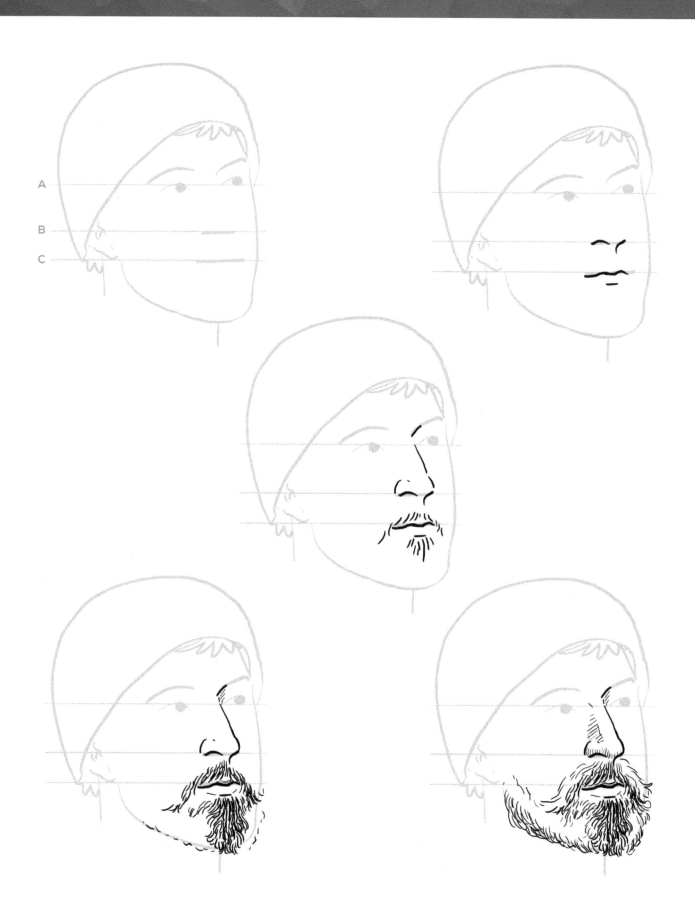

B

C

Expressions

The way to master drawing expressions is to understand that all facial features are connected by muscles. Grab a mirror and smile. Your mouth moves, but so do your cheeks. Squint, and your eyebrows will move and creases will show on your nose and brow.

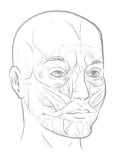 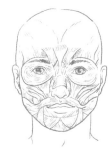 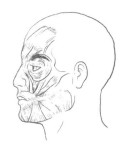

I slant and arch features depending on the expression. The more dramatic the slant, the more exaggerated the expression. To me, the eyebrows and mouth best express what someone is feeling.

   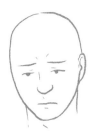 

The shape and size of features also vary according to expression. A mad face might have tight, thin lips, but someone laughing will have a mouth wide open, showing teeth. Someone sad will have eyes squinted shut, wrinkling the skin around them, but someone surprised will show more white of the eye and arch their brows toward their hairline.

  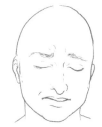 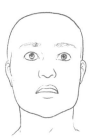

The easiest way to draw expressions is to use your own face as the model.

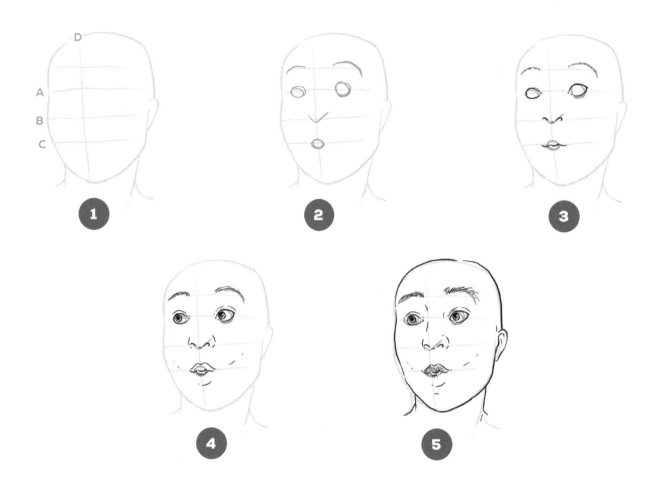

1 Let's draw a surprised face. First, lightly sketch a head with *ABCD* lines.

2 Draw the features. The eyes are round and fully open. The eyebrows are high. The mouth is pinched and slightly open, and the nostrils are slightly flared.

3 Define the features with a darker pencil. Draw the eyelids, dot where the eyebrows go, and draw the nostril holes and the start of the upper lip.

4 Finish the features. Because the eyes are so open, there is white above and below the iris. And since the mouth is stretched and slightly sucked in, the cheeks have hollows.

5 Define the chin, and add detail to the eyes, eyebrows, and bridge of the nose. Finally, draw the complete shape of the head.

Now that we've tried one together, practice a few on your own.
Remember, your portrait doesn't need to be perfect. Have fun!

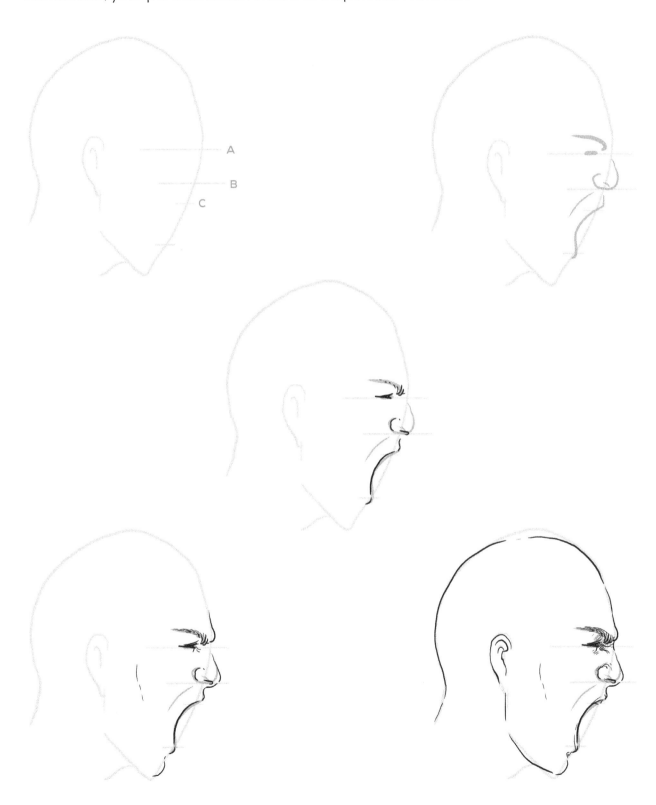

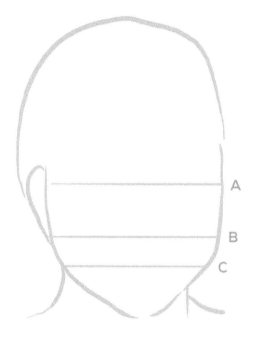

A

B

C

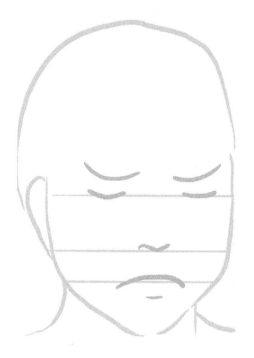

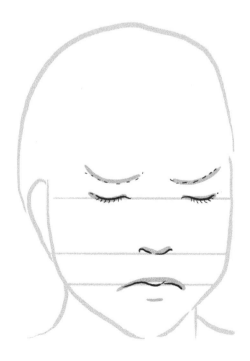

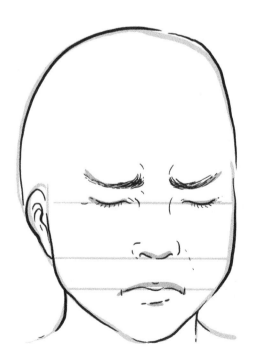

Part Two

THE DETAILS

Shading

WORDS TO LEARN

highlights: the lightest tones, almost white; use very light pen pressure or use an eraser to get back to white

tone: the intensity and saturation (richness) of color

shadows: the darkest tones; use heavy pen pressure

midtones: the color values between light and dark; use medium pen pressure

Let's add **tone**. Think of areas of the face as slopes that pop outward or sink inward.

The cheekbones, top of the nose, forehead, eyebrows, middle of the chin, and part of the upper lip stick out, so they catch light and have the most **highlights**. Other areas, like under the nose and lower lip and around the eyes, don't get as much light because they sink inward or have **shadows** cast on them from other features. Flat areas—near the hairline and around main features—get shaded with **midtones**.

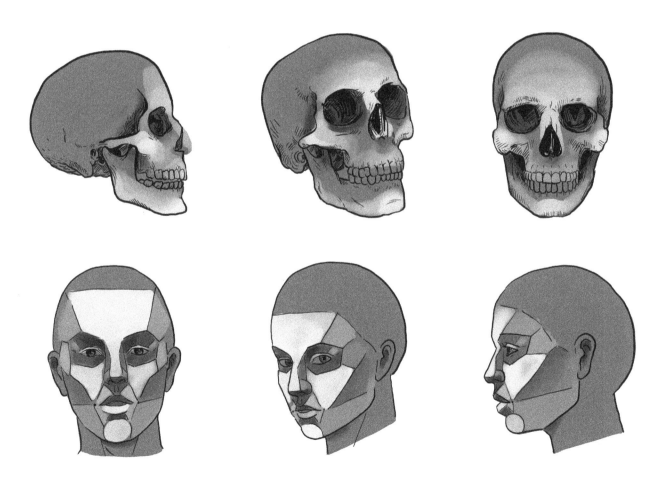

Pressing hard with a pencil produces a dark line, and pressing lightly produces a soft gray. You can use your finger to smudge shadows. When shading, don't change stroke direction; follow the direction of the skull slopes, such as the cheekbones curving in a \ / direction.

Most Pressure

Least Pressure

Shadows

Midtones

Highlights

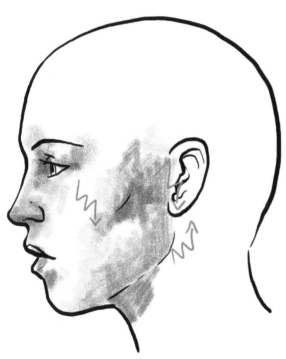

Don't change direction when shading.

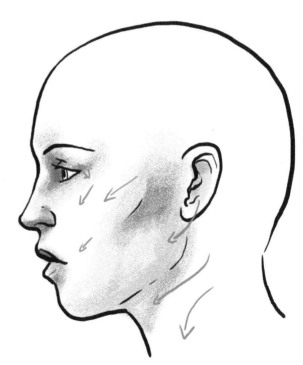

Follow the form and keep strokes consistent with direction and pressure.

Try lighting your subject strongly to see the contrast between light and dark. Lighting from one side makes a dramatic portrait. Lighting from the front means fewer shadows.

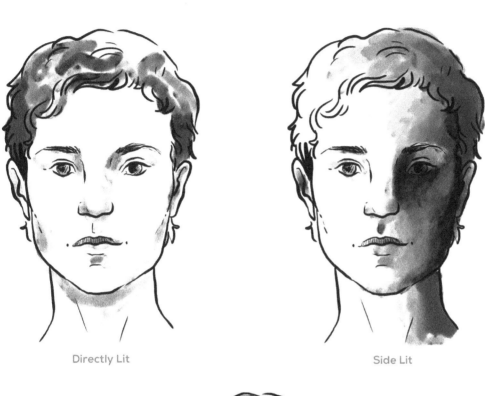

Directly Lit

Side Lit

Lit from Below

Lit from Above

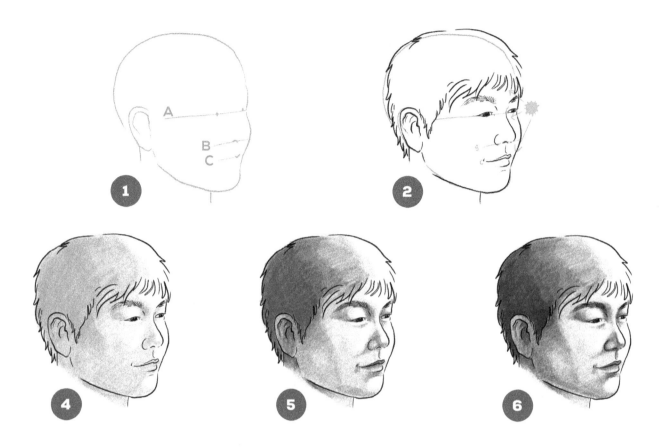

1   Lightly sketch a basic head shape with *ABC* lines.

2   Draw simple lines for the main features (eyes, nose, and lips). Here, the light is coming from the right, which means the left side will be mostly in shadow.

3   Lay down a broad, light shade where the shadow is cast: the side of the nose, left cheek, lips, eyes, and half of the chin.

4   Apply slightly more pressure with your pencil. Shade a bit darker under the cheekbone and the chin, the side of the nose, and the eye area.

5   Keep building up shadows and blend them. Add highlights of pure white (with chalk or white ink, or by erasing) on areas that catch light the best—the eyes, tip of the nose, and lips. This really brings a portrait to life.

Tip: Always work from light to dark. You can build shadow, but it's hard to lighten areas without erasing. Also, don't go super dark when shading, because the drawing can look overdone.

Now that we've tried one together, practice a few on your own. Remember, your portraits don't need to be perfect. Have fun!

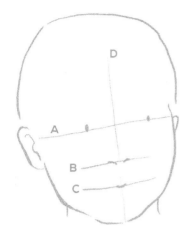

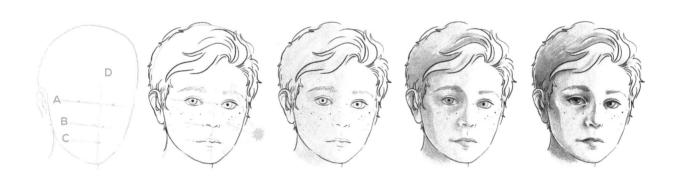

ACTIVITY SIX

Beyond the Face

Now for the finishing touches: hair, beards, necks, and ears, plus any individual characteristics, like scars, freckles, moles, and glasses. These details bring out the uniqueness of your subject.

When sketching hair, think of how light travels across the shape of the head. Where are the highlights? Roughly draw hair with thick, broad, sweeping strokes, and shade in the direction the hair is curling. After that, add a few thin marks for wisps of hair around the face and head. Apply the same method for beards and mustaches.

Ears come in many shapes and sizes and typically lie somewhere in between the eyebrow and mouth. Each ear is unique—they can have attached or free earlobes, be long or short, wide or narrow. They could have a variety of piercings, too!

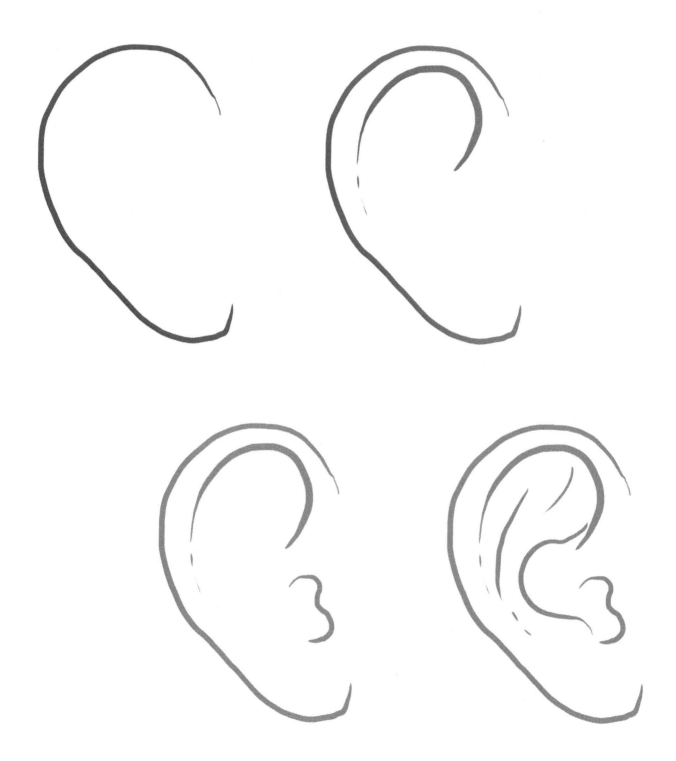

Necks connect to the head behind the earlobes. They come in different lengths and thicknesses and can have features like Adam's apples and beards.

Adam's Apple

Clavicle (Collarbone)

1   Lightly sketch a basic head with *ABCD* lines.

2   With a dark pencil, draw a simple portrait. Use dashes to show where the hair will go.

3   Start the ears between the eyes and lips. Draw a lopsided peanut shape, then draw the curve of the top of the ear and sideways C and M shapes. Start the shirt collar with a V shape. Sketch the glasses with dashed lines. Dash the hairline across the forehead.

4   For the hair, begin with short, dashes around the ears and the side of the head. Space them out more as you reach the top of the head, which is catching light.

5   Connect the dashed lines to form the glasses, then gradually thicken the line to make solid black frames. Frames often have the eyes at the center of the lenses, and they can cut off some of the eyebrows. Draw the outer ear and earlobes, then finish the shirt and add details, like his Adam's apple.

Now that we've tried one together, practice a few on your own.
Remember, it doesn't need to be perfect. Have fun!

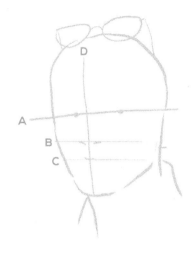

Your Selfie

WORDS TO LEARN

exposure: the amount of light in a photo; **overexposed** can be too bright, and **underexposed** can be too dark

Now it's time to take a selfie!

The best light to use is daylight. Avoid **overexposing** your face; try standing at an angle so that some light passes across your face. If it's night, use a warm white lightbulb, or for fun, use Christmas lights! Using the flash overexposes things.

Stretch your arm out and keep it at the same height as your face. Taking pictures when you're holding your camera up high can make your portrait look distorted. You can also try resting your device on a shelf and using its timer. This is great for action shots and group shots.

Try taking many selfies: Make different expressions, tilt your head in different ways, or move your arm around to capture different angles.

The most important thing? Relax and have fun. Try out crazy hats or put on fun makeup—treat this as your own mini photo shoot.

1 First, take a selfie! Be outside or near a light source to cast some shadow.

2 Print your selfie or look at it on your device for reference. Start with a light pencil head sketch with *ABCD* lines.

3 With a darker pencil or pen, sketch your eyes, nose, and lips. Draw a bit of your chin, neck, and shoulders, and dot where your hairline is.

4 Next, finish your facial features.

5 Draw some broad strokes for your hair, following the direction it flows.

6 Using your pencil, add some shadow with light-to-medium pressure.

   Tip: If the shadow is too light to see, you can use your device to edit it to increase the shadow, decrease the highlights, and pump up the contrast. You can also desaturate (lessen the intensity) or remove color with an app to make the photo black-and-white and simplify it.

Now that we've tried one together, practice a few on your own. Remember, it doesn't need to be perfect. Have fun!

Strike a Pose!

Grab a Friend!

Your Subject

Find a comfortable, well-lit place for your subject to sit, like a window with natural light. Don't ask them to do something tiring like holding an expression. They can listen to music, watch TV, or play with their phone; just ask them not to move their head too much.

Place paper on an easel or a table on your left, and position your model on your right. This way, you can glance back and forth rather than move your head up and down. Lightly sketch quick marks with as many details as you can, and try to get the overall face. Your lines don't have to be perfect. After 5 to 10 minutes, let your model take a break. If you get your sketch done before time runs out, start drawing darker lines and shadows to define the facial features.

A great place to find subjects is out in public. You can sketch people in restaurants, dog owners with their pets in a park, or kids eating lunch in the cafeteria.

- Grab some face paint and paint your subject as a character, like a clown or superhero.

- Pose your model in front of patterned wallpaper for a beautiful backdrop.

- Dress your model to match your pet, then draw a portrait of the two of them in a scene.

- Use only shades of one color for a **monochromatic** drawing. Or use shades of only two colors for a **bichromatic** piece.

- Look to myths and legends for inspiration. Draw mermaids or centaurs using your subject as the portrait reference.

- Find a subject who also likes to draw and draw each other drawing each other!

1   Set your timer and start with a light sketch of the basic head shape with *ABCD* lines.

2   Define the lips, nose, and eyes, and add movement to the hair. Because I'm making my model Rapunzel, I'm adding flowers, exaggerating her hair, and changing her outfit.

3   With a black pen, start drawing from the model. Focus on drawing everything you need from the model in front of you before your timer runs out.

4   Once finished, erase the sketch. Lightly draw where the shadows are. Give your model a short break and re-pose them after if you need to.

5   Once you're done with the model, finish the piece using your imagination. Detail all the flowers and her costume, and add the shadows with pencil.

Now that we've tried one together, practice a few on your own. Remember, it doesn't need to be perfect. Have fun!

The Profile

WORDS TO LEARN

silhouette: the dark shape or outline of someone or something against a lighter background

The side view of a person is a great way to see their defining features.
Here are some common mistakes when drawing profiles:

- squishing the back of the head and forgetting there's a big brain back there

- forgetting that from the side, the eyes look more like **>** than a nut shape

- extending features too far out

- forgetting that lips and nostrils are three-dimensional and stick out from the face

Remember: Features don't lie flat. Your face indents (dips in) between your eyebrows and eyes, between your upper and lower lips, and between your lips and chin. It protrudes (sticks out) at your brows, nose, and lips.

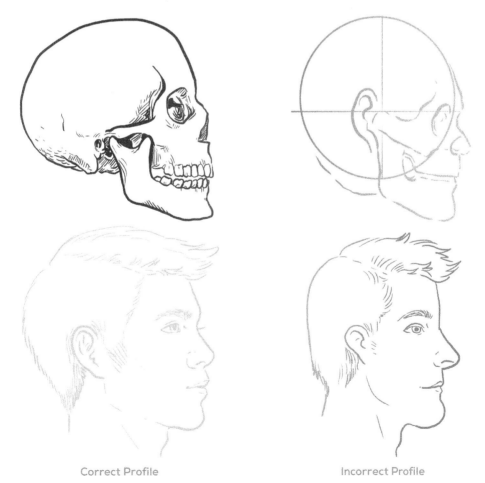

Correct Profile   Incorrect Profile

Before cameras, people who wanted affordable portraits of their loved ones made **silhouette** drawings. Once cameras were invented, this tradition died out, but recently it's had a comeback. You can take silhouette portraits a step further by using decorative paper instead of black or adding embellishments like rhinestones or gold leaf.

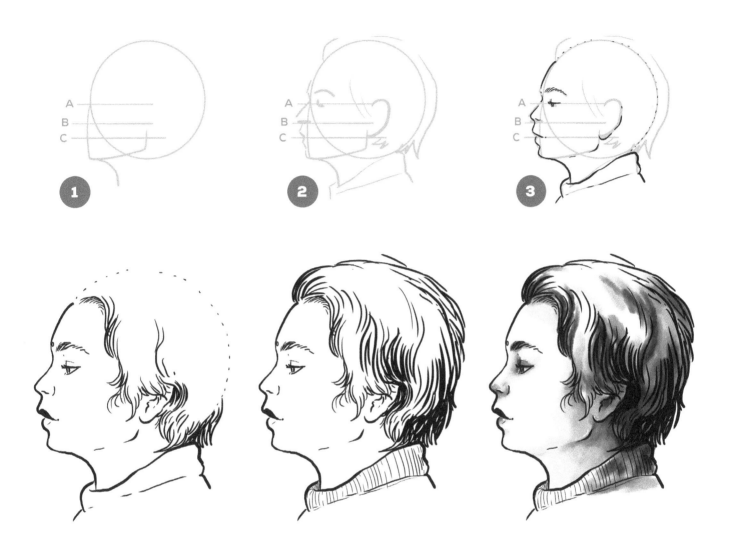

1   Pencil a circle for the skull, a curved triangle for the jaw, and *ABC* lines.

2   Sketch the indents and where the nose, lips, and brows reach out from the skull. Draw the ear and indicate the hairline.

3   With a dark marker, start your final line drawing on top of your sketch. Focus on just the face's outline. Then, start drawing some details.

4   Finish the face's details and start the hair. Using large strokes, show the direction of the hair and its darker areas.

5   Finish with some thin, fine lines for the hair. Then finish the outfit.

6   With pencil or watercolor (if your marker is waterproof), add shadow or color.

Now that we've tried one together, practice a few on your own. Remember, it doesn't need to be perfect. Have fun!

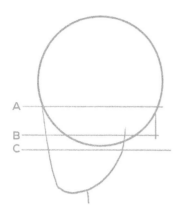
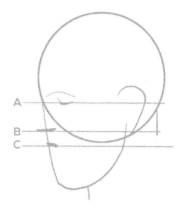

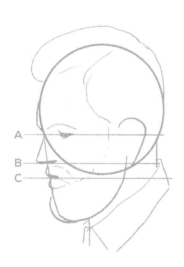
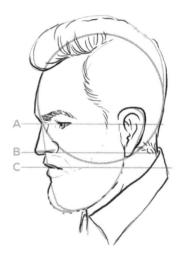

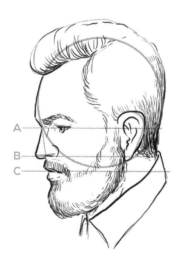

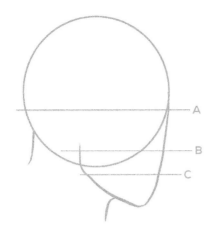

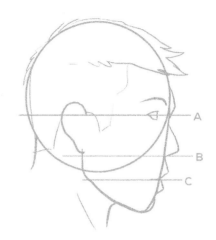

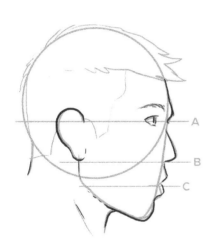

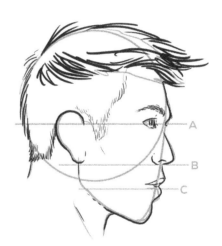

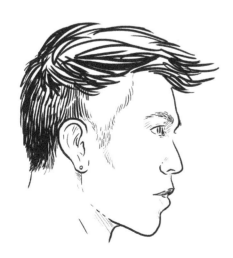

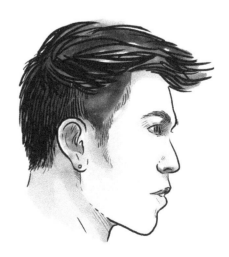

Portraits Through the Ages

Girl with a Pearl Earring by Johannes Vermeer

Portrait paintings through the ages have had a huge range of media and styles. In the ancient world, artists created portraits on papyrus scrolls in Egypt, pottery in Greece and Rome, and block prints and ink paintings in Japan and China.

Stela of Saiah

Portrait of a young woman in red

Three Beauties of the Present Day by Kitagawa Utamaro

John the Baptist (John in the Wilderness) by Caravaggio

The Reader by Jean-Honore Fragonard

Portrait of a Lady by Gustav Klimt

1400 to 1600: **Italian Renaissance.** Artists like Leonardo da Vinci and Caravaggio used **chiaroscuro** to make almost photo-realistic portraits done in oil and egg tempera.

1700s: **Rococo.** During this period, there were lighter, airier paintings full of color, high fashion, and rough brushstrokes, like in Jean-Honoré Fragonard's *The Reader*.

Late 1800s to early 1900s: **Art Nouveau.** During this period, the style shifted to more graphic and decorative work like those done by artists Gustav Klimt and Alphonse Mucha.

Camille Monet and a Child in the Artist's Garden in Argenteuil by Claude Monet

Late 1800s to early 1900s: **Impressionism.** Artists tried to capture an impression rather than an exact copy during this time. Famous painters from this period include Vincent van Gogh and Claude Monet.

Woman with a Hat by Henri Matisse

Early 1900s: **Fauvism**. This period was similar in style to Impressionism but was rougher and wilder with vivid colors, as in the work of Henri Matisse.

1900 to the 1950s: **Expressionism**. Twisted forms and strong colors used to recreate emotions were the focus of this period. **Cubism** centered on creating flat, two-dimensional paintings using geometric shapes, like in the work of Pablo Picasso. **Surrealism** had strange, thought-provoking pieces taken from the subconscious mind, like in the work of Salvador Dalí and René Magritte.

Today: Artists work in collage, paint, ink, graffiti, and digital, often drawing inspiration from the past.

The Old Guitarist by Pablo Picasso

Let's draw in the style of ancient Greek pottery:

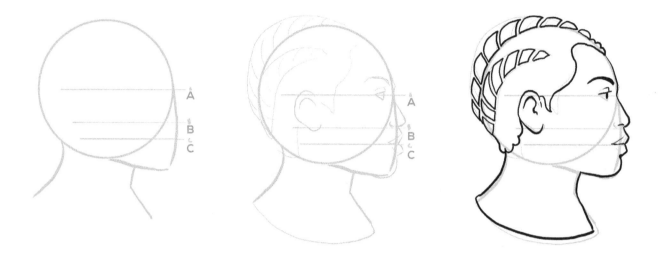

1   With an orange pencil, draw a basic head shape with *ABC* lines.

2   Lightly sketch the major facial features. The portraits on ancient pottery are very simple, so don't go into much detail.

3   With waterproof ink or marker, draw the outline. Create a decorative hairstyle. Again, keep it simple.

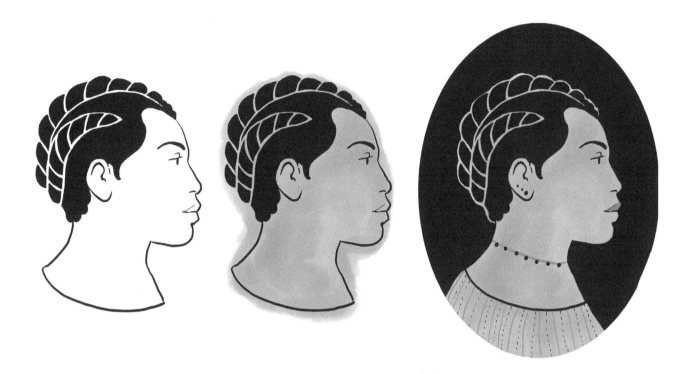

4   Fill in the black of the hair.

5   Color in and around the portrait.

6   Put the portrait in an oval shape. I extended her shoulders and colored the background black. I kept an orange outline around the hair to show off the braid details. Add some decorative lines with a darker orange.

Women outdoors,
attributed to Chrysis Painter Ink,
watercolor, or
colored pencil

Now that we've tried one together, practice a few on your own. Remember, it doesn't need to be perfect. Have fun!

Pencil or charcoal, white chalk, and tinted paper

The Head of the Virgin in Three-Quarter View Facing Right by Leonardo da Vinci

Chalk on brown paper or pastel paints

Self-Portrait with a Straw Hat
by Vincent van Gogh

The Modern Selfie

Contemporary artists have a wide range of visual styles. Andy Warhol drew **graphic** portraits with pops of color. Chuck Close made grids and placed tiny patterns within each square, which from a distance form a portrait. Kehinde Wiley creates intricate and detailed patterns with portraits bursting from them. Amy Sherald plays with both color and **grayscale**, and Ralph Steadman uses quick, loose ink strokes, often spilling ink and paint over his canvas to make excitingly wild pieces. Yuko Shimizu's pieces are a blend of traditional Japanese illustration and modern-day comics.

So don't worry about being perfect! Let's use new materials, like paint, watercolor, and pastels, and have fun with color. You want to make your portrait's hair blue? Do it! If you're looking for inspiration, now's the time to break out your phone and turn on those filters.

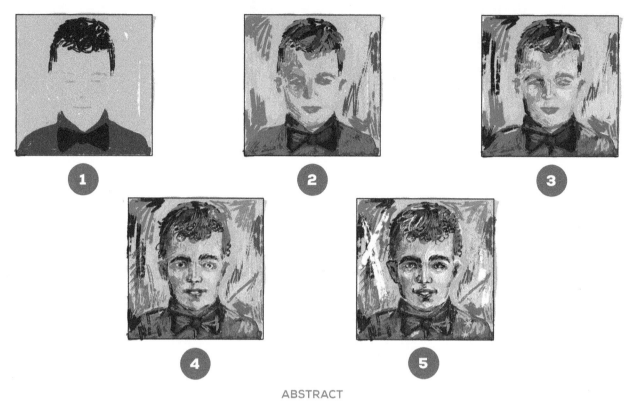

ABSTRACT

Canvas or board base, acrylic paint, brushes, water, and paper towels

1   Gather a mix of acrylic paint; a canvas or board made for paint; large, medium, and small paintbrushes; paper towels; and a cup of water. Cover the floor with newspaper, and paint the basic shapes of the head and outfit and a solid background.

2   Use a medium brush to begin the facial features. Think of areas in shadow as blues and purples and highlighted areas as yellows, oranges, and reds. Do some **drybrushing** to create textures. Clean your paintbrush by dipping it in water and wiping it with a paper towel when you switch colors. Smear extra color from your brush onto that abstract background.

3   Keep adding color and build up the face. Use big, loose brushstrokes.

4   Use a medium brush to keep building colors and form. Add to the facial features. Increase the highlights and shadows.

5   Using the smaller brush, add details. Use a dark color to draw some clean lines for the facial features. Add highlights of white and red for some "pop." Flick the brush to splatter some random dots!

Now that we've tried one together, practice a few on your own. Remember, it doesn't need to be perfect. Have fun!

WARHOL

A dried black marker, a regular black marker, and colored markers

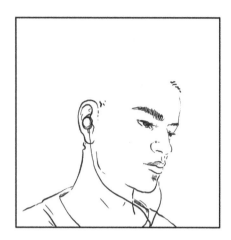

WATERCOLOR

Waterproof ink, watercolor paper, watercolors, brushes, water, and paper towels

POP ART

Canvas or board, acrylic paint, brushes, water, and paper towels

Group Portrait

Group portraits need a bit more planning than portraits with an individual. Start by lightly sketching everyone first, and make sure you position them in a nice arrangement on your paper. You don't want to squish them all together or draw them too small. When sketching, lightly draw ovals for their heads and arches for their shoulders; that way you can quickly draw and erase until your piece looks right to you. Once you've finished that, you can place your *ABCD* lines. Finally, I suggest drawing each portrait one at a time.

   For this activity, I recommend using a photo for reference. It's easier to have it on hand than to try to pose everyone as an individual or pose the group for a long period. Keep backgrounds simple to focus attention on the faces.

1   For each individual, start by blocking in the basic shapes of the head and upper body very lightly with pencil. Sketch where the eyes, nose, and mouth will go.

2   Sketch slightly darker the details of the hair, clothing, and facial features.

3   With ink, start finishing the portrait and body of one figure. Then finish the other figures.

4   Erase the sketch and add any final details and shadows.

Now that we've tried one together, practice a few on your own. Remember, it doesn't need to be perfect. Have fun!

FURTHER READING

Anatomy of Facial Expression by Uldis Zarins with Sandis Kondrats. This book delves into the individual muscles of the face and how they're connected and goes very deep into how that impacts expressions.

Art: Over 2500 Works from Cave to Contemporary by Nigel Ritchie. A great collection of art and different styles throughout history.

Artists: Their Lives and Works by DK and Ross King. A collection of artists and their self-portraits, showing different selfies over time.

Authentic Portraits by Chris Orwig. Do you have a lot of fun taking photos of yourself and other people? This book goes into detail on capturing someone's soul and character through photography.

Drawing the Head and Hands by Andrew Loomis. An oldie but a goodie. Loomis teaches some classic academic lessons on portraits but goes into detail on matters such as facial structures.

How to Draw Comics the Marvel Way by Stan Lee and John Buscema. Take what you've learned in this book and apply it to making your own comics full of superheroes and villains.

Modern Art: A History from Impressionism to Today by Hans Werner Holzwarth. See some of the more modern and abstract ways artists in recent history have made portraits.

Norman Rockwell: 332 Magazine Covers by Christopher Finch. Rockwell was an iconic painter who captured memorable stories in his characters.

Portraits: A History by Andreas Beyer. A great collection of the different ways portraits have been made throughout art history.

The Artist's Complete Guide to Drawing the Head by William Maughan. For more advanced portrait artists, this book goes into drawing realistic portraits using just form and value.

The Atlas of Beauty: Women of the World in 500 Portraits by Mihaela Noroc. If you really love photography or just want to be inspired by the diversity of the world, this book captures the portraits of 500 women from across the globe.

INDEX

ABOUT THE AUTHOR

Angela Rizza graduated from the Fashion Institute of Technology in New York City in 2011 and since then has been creating artwork in Mahopac, New York. Her work is inspired by the wildlife around her home and her favorite childhood stories. She enjoys teaching art and creating activity books that help others learn and use their imagination.

CPSIA information can be obtained
at www.ICGtesting.com
Printed in the USA
JSHW051451140821
17811JS00001B/3

Figure Drawing
for Kids

FIGURE DRAWING
for kids

A Step-by-Step Guide to Drawing People

Angela Rizza

ROCKRIDGE PRESS

Interior and Cover Designer: Jami Spittler
Art Producer: Janice Akerman
Editor: Natasha Yglesias
Production Manager: Oriana Siska
Production Editor: Melissa Edeburn

Interior Photography: p. 66: Lucas Ottone/Stocksy.com; p. 67: VISUALSPECTRUM/Stocksy.com; p. 68: ZOA PHOTO/Stocksy.com; p. 69: sasar/istock.com; p. 70: MPH Photos/Shutterstock.com; p. 71: William87/istock.

Illustrations © Angela Rizza, 2019

ISBN: Print 978-1-64152-771-2 | Ebook 978-1-64611-812-0

R0

This book is dedicated to my grandparents, John and Martha Leone, who bought me my first drawing desks and art supplies and who inspired me to pursue art and always work on getting better.

CONTENTS

We learn from failure,
not from success!

-Bram Stoker

INTRODUCTION

Hello, budding artists! When I was your age, I used to doodle from how-to-draw books. With time and practice (and those helpful books), I grew up to be an illustrator. If you want to be an artist when you grow up, or if you're just looking for something fun and creative to do, this book can help.

It's easy to feel overwhelmed by illustrations in books and think you can't draw anything similar. I don't want you feeling that way, so I've broken the drawings in this book into simple steps, with plenty of verbal and visual tips. And don't worry, nothing you draw has to be perfect! Your first few drawings may not look exactly as you intended, but remember that nobody learns without making mistakes, trying new things, and leaping outside of their comfort zone.

I've given you a range of fun characters to draw. I want you to learn how to draw the human form, but also humanity. Thinking about your subjects as real people will make your art beautiful. Some of the figures in the book are inspired by my friends and family. Maybe a few resemble *your* friends or people you see around you. We deserve to truly see ourselves and others in our art, and I hope this book serves that goal.

Go at your own pace. If you feel like redoing an activity before moving on to the next, that's totally fine. Maybe there's one drawing you're having trouble with. You can always skip it for now and try it again another time. Drawing should feel fun, not like work!

I hope this book inspires you as much as the art books that inspired me.

HOW TO USE THIS BOOK

Each activity starts with a brief lesson and step-by-step drawings to show you the process to help you learn by seeing examples. Think of your drawings as practice. Don't feel pressured to make an exact copy of my drawings. Feel free to use the activities as guidance, and if you feel like changing a figure's hair or outfit, or adding your own unique touch, do it. Unleash your creativity!

The materials you'll need are affordable and easily available. There's no need to buy an easel or the most expensive pens—I sure didn't. Here are some supplies I used in creating the activities, but you don't need them all. You can start out with a pencil, an eraser, and a sketchpad.

- Pencils

- Erasers

- Sketchpad or sketchbook: Mixed-media paper can take lots of erasing, markers, ink, and watercolors. A good size is 8.5x11 inches.

- Ink pens: Micron, Pentel, Sharpie fine points, or classic black Magic Marker

- Colored pencils: Prismacolor pencils are a great investment.

- Colorful markers

- Crayons

- Watercolor palette and brushes: You don't need lots of different colors, because you can make any color with the primary colors: red, yellow, and blue. Red and yellow make orange, red and blue make purple, blue and yellow make green, and so on.

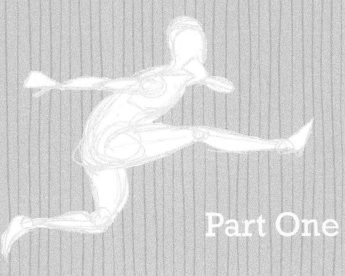

Part One

THE BASICS

Basic Shapes

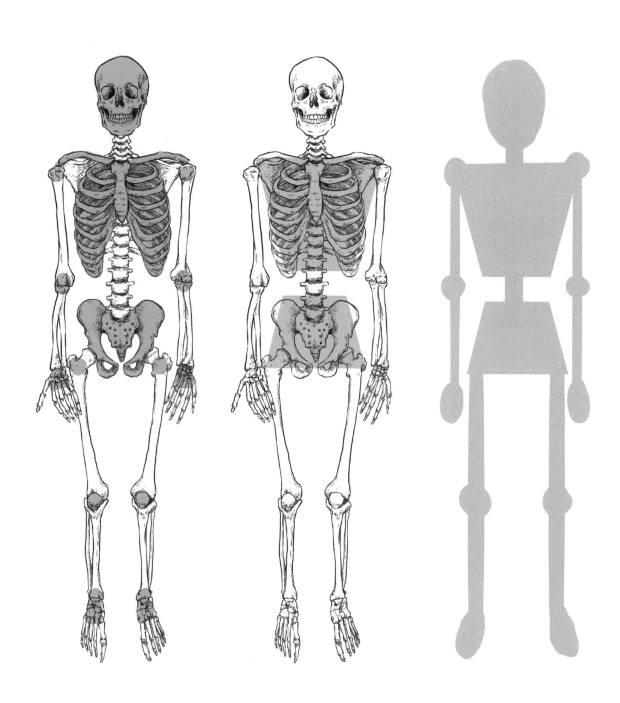

It's hard to draw a figure without understanding the human form underneath the clothes.

The human body has more than 200 bones and 650 muscles, but we'll focus on those most important for showing form and movement. We'll start with a stick figure and give it straight arms and legs. Let's make the torso an upside down trapezoid and the hips a right-side up trapezoid.

You can change the figure's pose and attitude by changing the angles of the hips and shoulders. For example, parallel lines will give you a still, standing figure, whereas lines slanting in opposite directions give your figure more life.

Next, connect the trapezoids to form a torso. Use sausage-like tubes to connect shoulders to elbows to hands, and hips to knees to feet. Play with the length and size of these shapes to create unique characters.

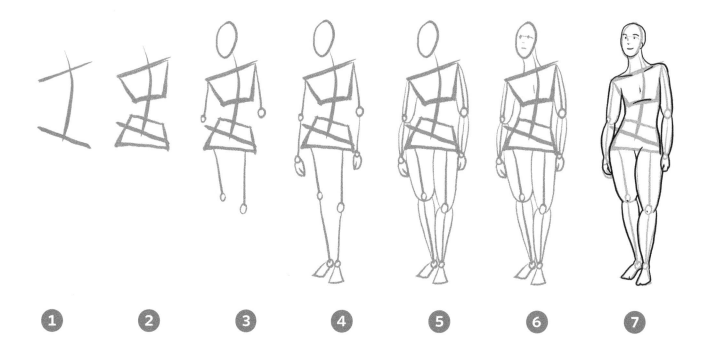

1 Begin by drawing lines for the shoulders and hips. Connect them with a line for the spine. Curving the spine gives the figure movement and life.

2 Lightly sketch trapezoids for the hips and ribs.

3 Next, add upper arm and thigh lines. The left shoulder is drooping, so the left elbow will be lower. The right hip is drooping, so the right knee will be lower.

4 Now connect the form to the limbs.

5 Use the sausage shapes to draw forearms, hands, shins, and feet.

6 Connect the trapezoids to create a waist, then draw the neck and head.

7 Use a black marker or pen to outline the whole body and see your first figure!

Now that we've tried one together, practice a few on your own. Remember, it doesn't need to be perfect. Have fun!

Using a Grid

Using a grid can help us draw a figure. We can use "heads" as a measurement for height. The average height of an adult is 8 heads. Generally, the elbows and belly button are 3 heads down, and the hands and mid-thigh area are 5 heads down.

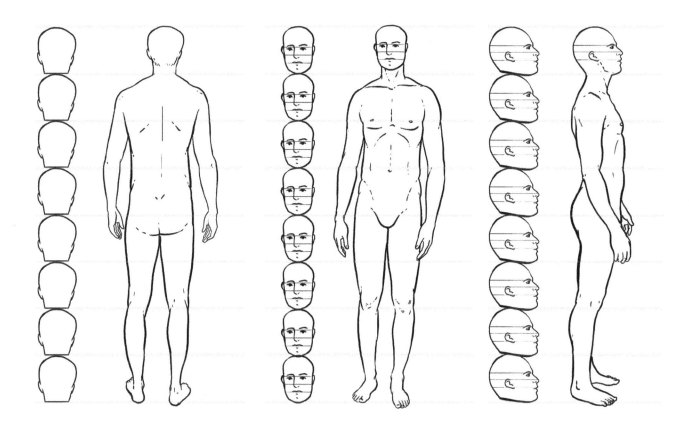

WORDS TO LEARN

proportion: the relationship between
the size of one thing and another

By changing the number of heads, we can draw different figures. A figure 4 heads tall
could be a toddler, a figure 7 heads tall could be a senior citizen (we shrink with age),
and a figure 9 heads tall could be a comic book hero.

If we turn the grid on an angle, we can draw a figure standing sideways or three-quarters of the way and still keep its **proportion**.

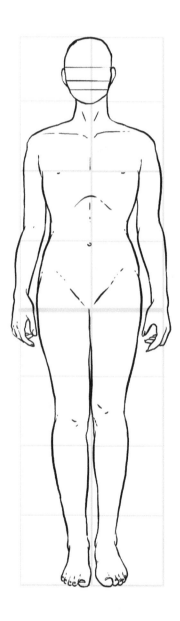
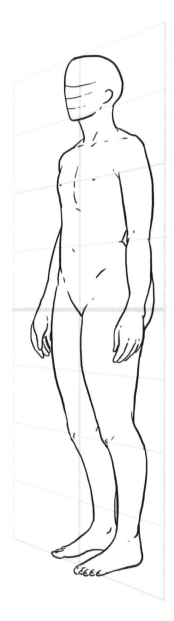
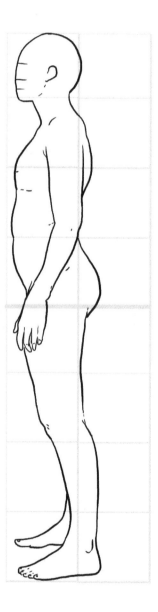

We can even use grids to draw seated figures by shifting the boxes with the knees over slightly to the right. Then we can draw new lines to connect the knees to the thighs.

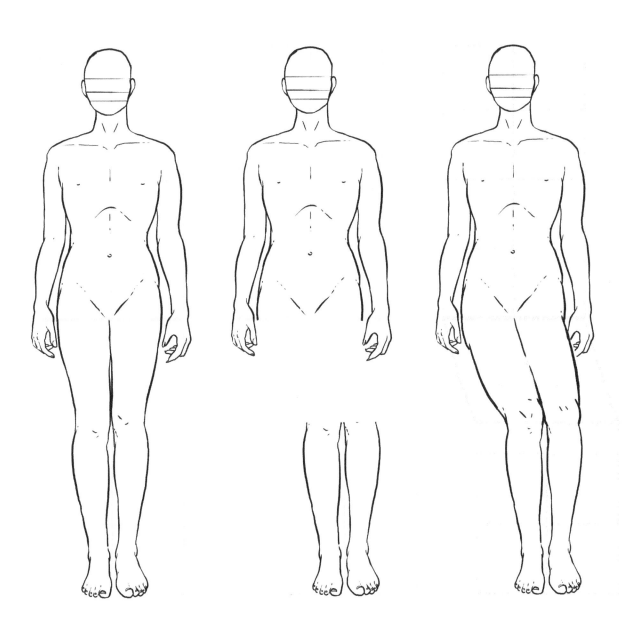

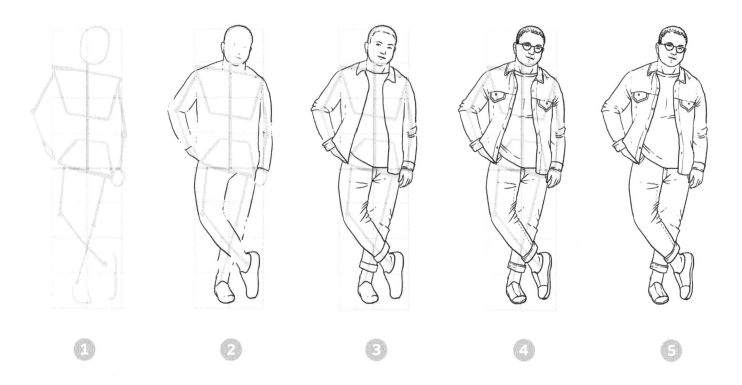

1. We'll make an 8-head figure, so draw 8 rows of 2 equal boxes to create a grid. The head fits in the top row, and the spine lines up with the center line. The shoulders and hips are mostly inside the grid, but it's okay if arms and legs are a little bit outside.

2. Time for the outline. Drawing little dashes in some areas means you can draw clothing folds later without having to erase a bunch of solid lines.

3. Finish the outline. Add little squiggles for clothing folds where you drew dashes. Add some lines to represent clothing. This figure wears a jacket, a T-shirt, and jeans. You can copy this or dress him differently.

4. Finish your figure with a few more details.

5. Erase the sketch lines.

Now that we've tried one together, practice a few on your own. Remember, it doesn't need to be perfect. Have fun!

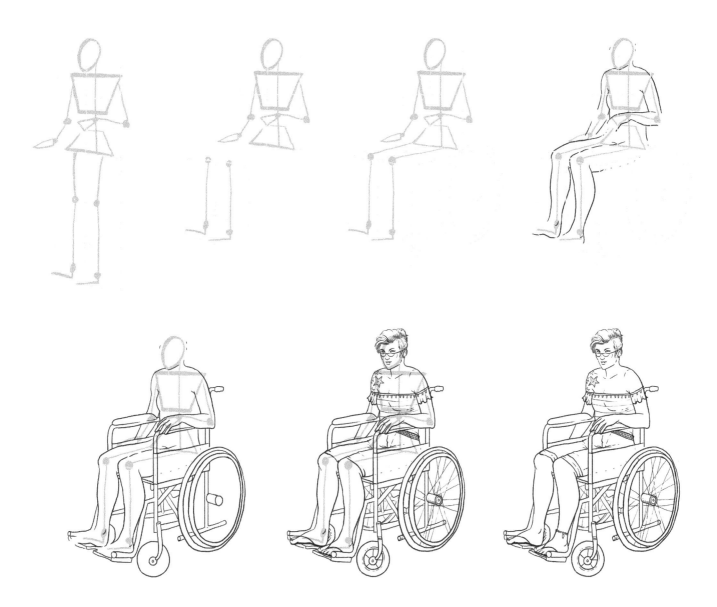

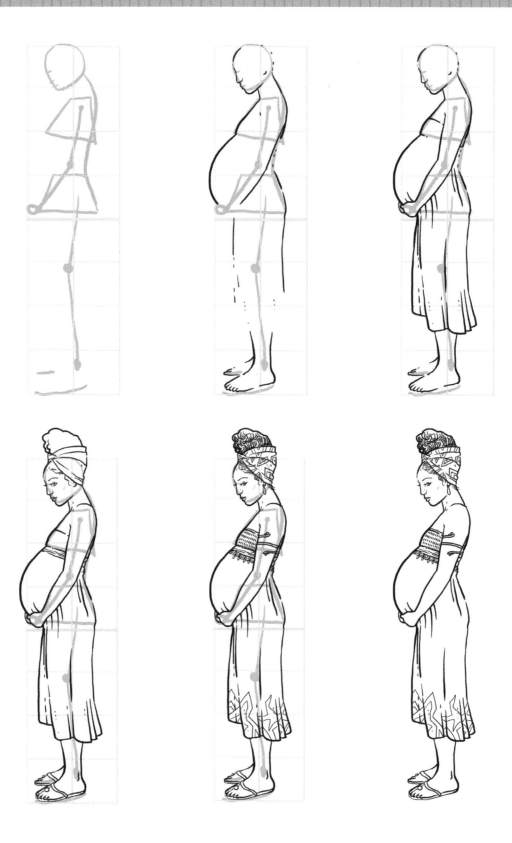

Defining the Body

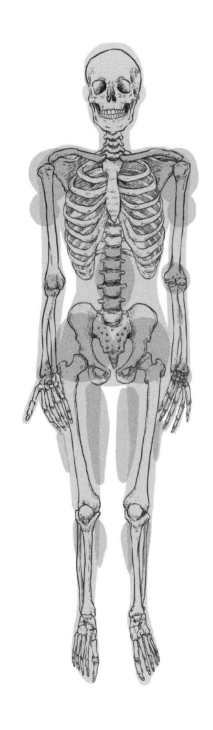
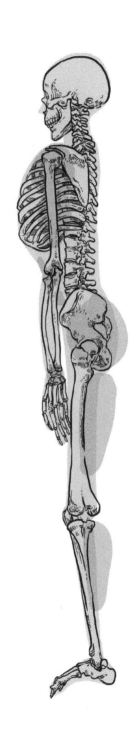

Let's expand on our skeleton from activity 1 (page 2). The blue area on the previous page is the basic shape, and the red areas are some important muscles. The size of the red areas can be different. Some bodies carry a lot of muscle in their chest, shoulders, and biceps, and their backs and chests are broad. Other bodies might have less-muscled arms but larger, rounder hips. Children often have little muscle, and babies are often round with baby fat.

   If muscles are working, they will be more noticeable and more defined. The back of someone resting looks pretty flat, but if they do a pull-up, you'll see those back muscles working. The more you keep this consideration in mind, the more detailed your figures can be.

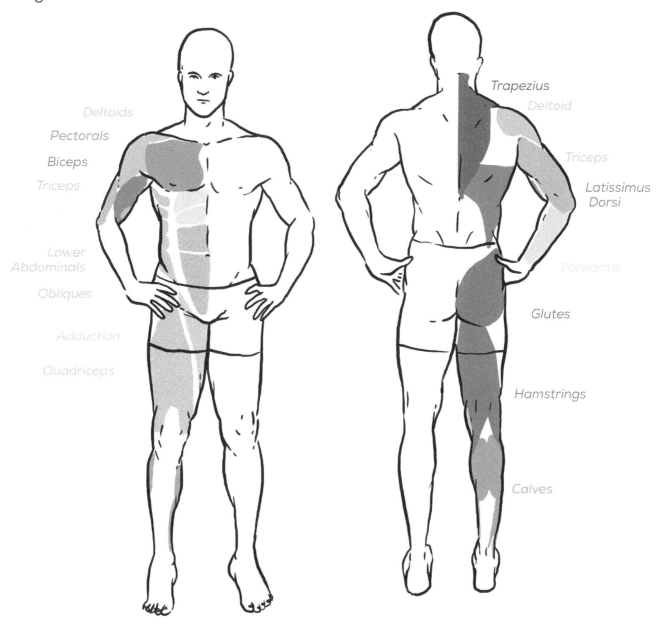

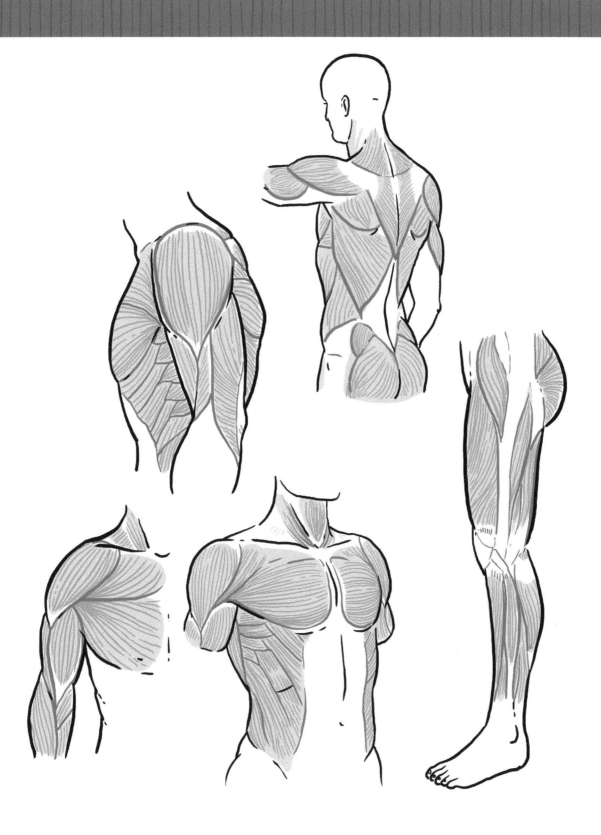

Try It Out

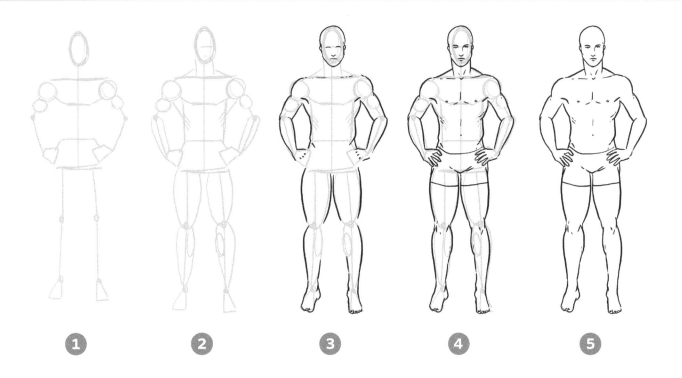

1. Start with a basic stick figure with boxy hips and chest. Add two circles in the upper arms for deltoids and biceps.

2. Finish the form with oval shapes for limbs, then add some circles inside the lower legs for calves. Connect the arms a bit lower on the torso, near the ribs to give the figure a broad back and an athletic look.

3. Next, draw the outline.

4. Add a bit of a curve to areas like the calves and upper arms to help show the muscles. You can also add detail to the chest and knees. Where major muscles connect, we can see small creases through the skin. You can show them with little dots and dashes.

5. Finish the figure by erasing your sketch lines.

   TIP:
   For these kinds of details, less is more!

Now that we've tried one together, practice a few on your own. Remember, your figures don't need to be perfect. Have fun!

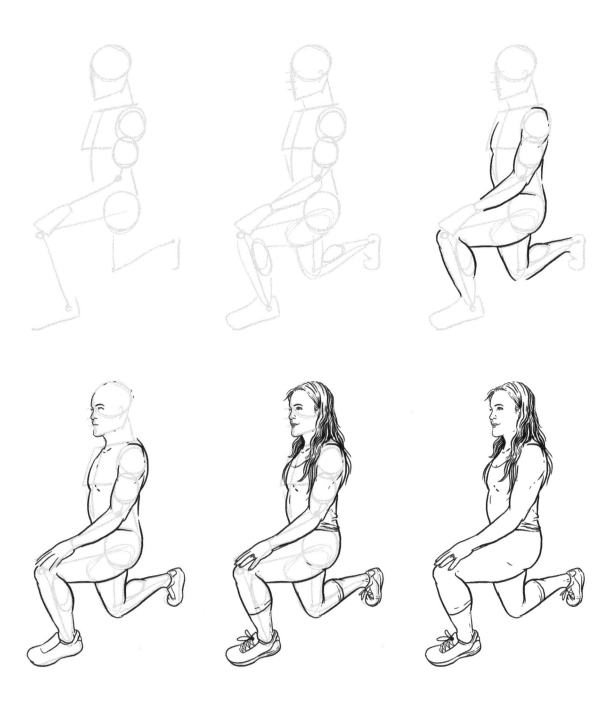

ACTIVITY FOUR

Ghosting

Figure Drawing for Kids

Ghosting is a way of looking at a figure as a whole shape.

Begin with a very light shade of pencil. Draw trapezoids for the torso, a circle for the head, and lines for the legs and arms. Thicken the lines for the upper arms and legs, then use slightly thinner shapes for the lower limbs. Think of the figure as **positive space** and the area around it as **negative space**.

Once you've finished the "ghost," you should have a shadow figure. Now you can add shapes or line art to build up the form.

1. Start by drawing the chest and hips of your ghost with a light shade. Next, make the pose of the arms with simple lines and a basic outline for the dress.

2. Fill out the figure, adding muscle and clothing. Remember the positive space in the gaps!

3. With a darker color, draw the main lines of the figure. Start defining the face and muscle in places such as the shoulders and legs.

4. Add detail, such as major folds in clothing and their portrait, or likeness.

5. Now have fun! I gave my figure a floral dress, a tattoo, and jewelry. You can do the same or something new.

Now that we've tried one together, practice a few on your own. Remember, your figures don't need to be perfect. Have fun!

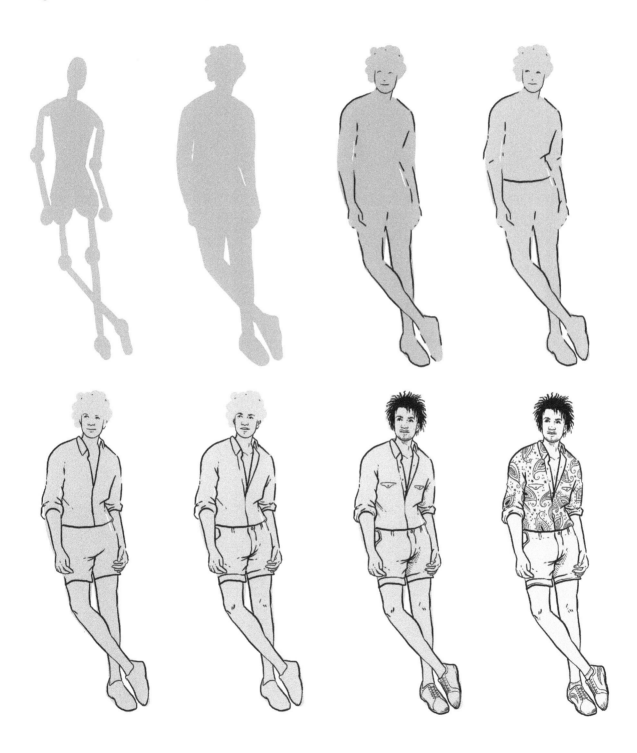

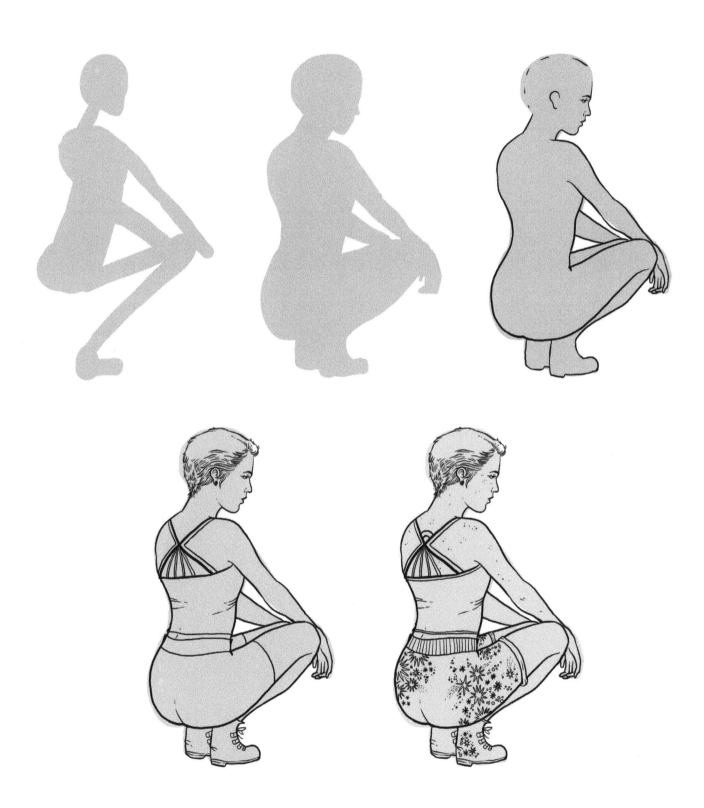

ACTIVITY FIVE

Movement

WORDS TO LEARN

parallel: two side-by-side lines the same distance apart

horizontal: a straight line that runs left to right

arch: a curved line

Now let's make our figures lively!

A still, standing figure has its feet directly under the head, hands at its sides, and shoulders and hips **parallel**. As the body shifts from one foot to the other, knees and elbows bend, and the spine becomes an **arch**.

When drawing movement, imagine yourself doing the same activity as the figure. Will you lower your hips? In which direction is your back bending? Will your weight be forward or backward? Which foot is bearing more weight?

Start with the basic stick form and don't focus on accuracy. Make quick, rough lines, exaggerating the pose to really show what's happening. After that, start adding shape. Then finish by drawing any final detail lines.

1. In light pencil, sketch the head and body, then add arms and legs. Pay attention to the curve of the spine. Remember, you can use a grid.

2. Use short dashed lines for the main body parts. My figure is in a skirt, so just draw enough leg to know what's there. Then finish drawing the basic body shape outfit, and add details for her face, fingers, elbows, and skirt.

3. Add details for her hair and portrait. Connect the skirt folds with a curved line. The more curves you add in the fabric, the more motion you'll show.

4. Now have fun! Because she is arching backward, her hair is being tossed behind her. Curls add movement. Then add detail to her outfit.

5. Finish the figure by erasing your sketch lines.

Now that we've tried one together, practice a few on your own. Remember, your figures don't need to be perfect. Have fun!

Point of View

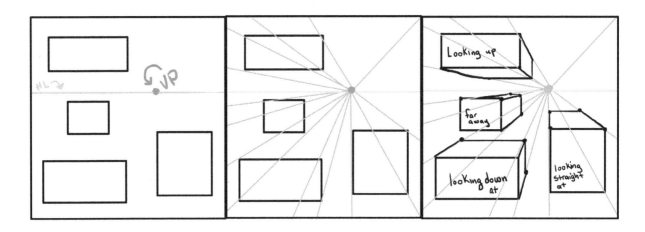

WORDS TO LEARN

point of view: the place or position from which an artist sees their subject

vanishing point: a point in an image where all perspective lines join

horizon line: a line across the page that represents the viewer's eye level

foreshortening: playing with the size in a drawing to show distance or proportion

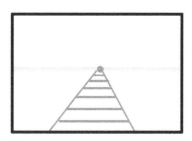 

So far, we've drawn figures standing at the same level as us. But what happens when we look down from a higher position? What happens when we look up at a figure from below? These examples highlight **point of view**.

   Imagine train tracks. The farther the tracks go into the distance, the closer together they seem to become. Eventually they seem to meet. That point in the distance is the **vanishing point**. It rests on the **horizon line**, a line that stretches across the page from left to right. Imagine you're looking at the ocean. Where the water and sky meet is the horizon line, and raising or lowering it can change our viewpoint.

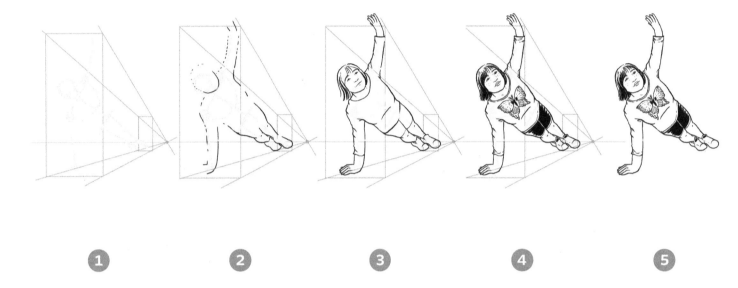

1 Let's put our figure in a box. Draw a horizon line and mark the vanishing point. Next, draw a tall rectangle to hold the head and shoulders. Closer to the vanishing point, draw a smaller rectangle for the feet. Connect the corners of the rectangles to the vanishing point.

2 Draw a stick figure in your box. The limbs are **foreshortened** and shorter than usual because they're far away. Draw the outline of the figure in dashes. Try drawing what's closest to you first.

3 Now build on those dashes, adding major lines and some clothing.

4 Finish the clothing and add details. The head and shoulders will have the most details because they are closest, and the legs and feet will have fewer because they're farther away. Complete the figure's portrait and outfit.

5 Finish the figure by erasing the sketch lines.

Now that we've tried one together, practice a few on your own. Remember, your figures don't need to be perfect. Have fun!

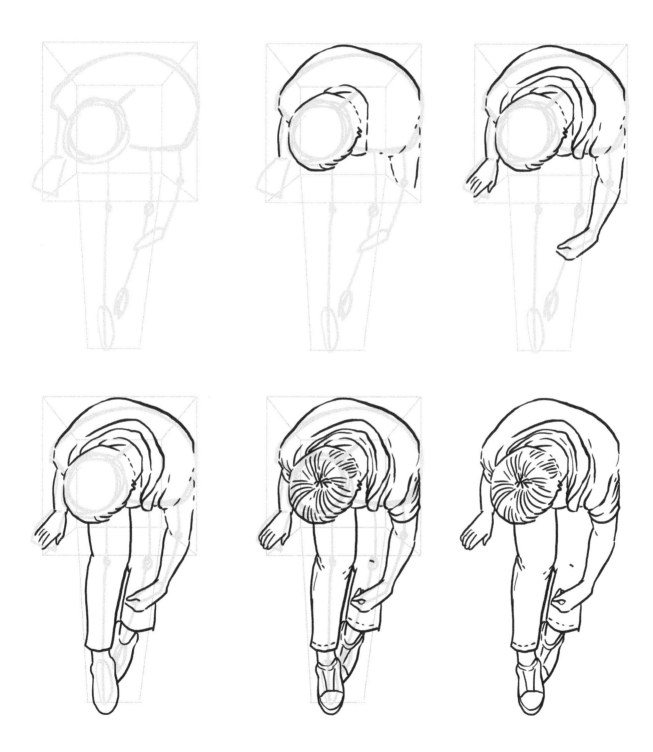

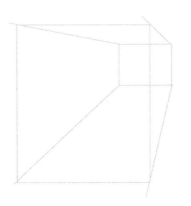
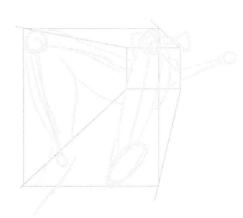

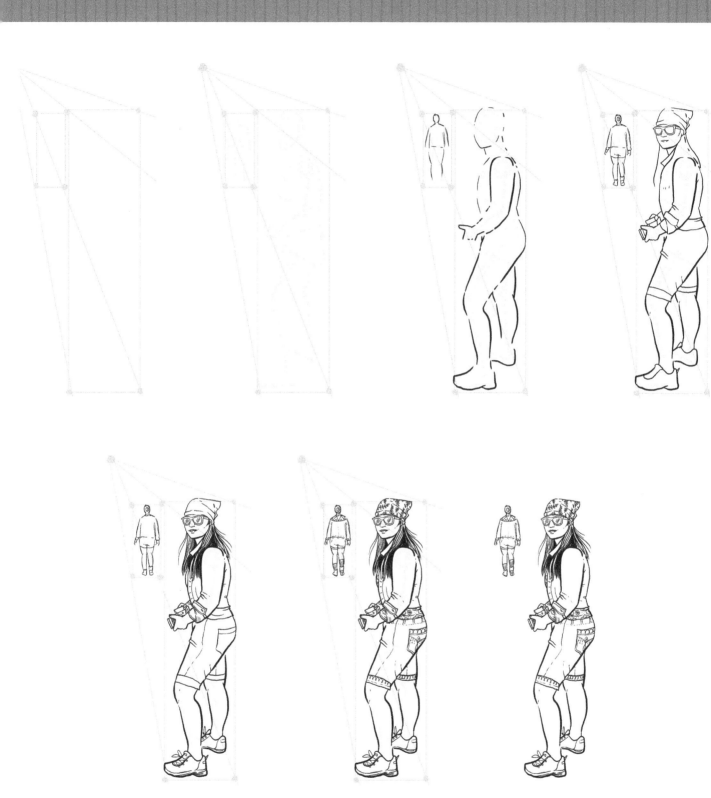

Part Two

THE DETAILS

Shading

There's more to shading than just adding black! Shadows can be angular or round, hard or soft, and they help set a mood. They can jump from light to dark or gradually darken with many **midtones**.

In line art, figures can appear flat. Shading helps them appear more three dimensional. When shading, start out lightly and slowly apply more pressure as you move into your darkest **value**.

There are many ways to shade. In this activity, we'll use different mediums to learn how shading can add to our drawings. Grab a pencil, pen, or even some watercolors, and let's get started!

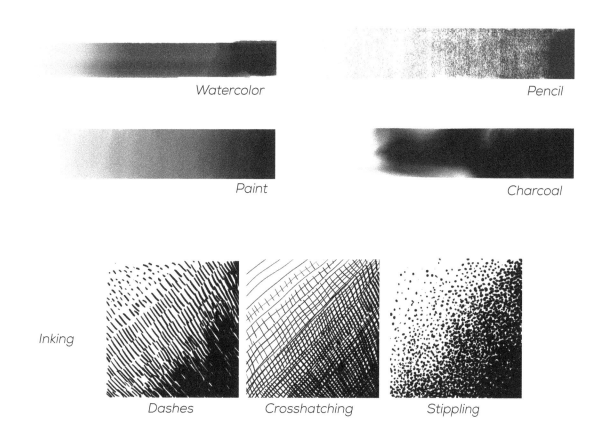

Watercolor

Pencil

Paint

Charcoal

Inking

Dashes

Crosshatching

Stippling

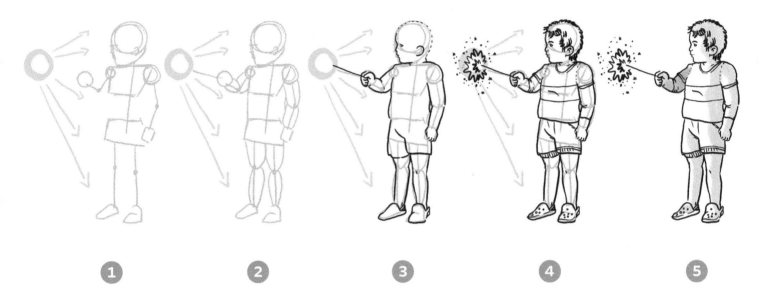

1 Gather a pencil, a waterproof marker or pen, an eraser, watercolors, a brush, a cup of water, and a paper towel. Lightly sketch in pencil a skeleton for this boy holding a sparkler.

2 Next, add ovals and circles to create a fuller figure.

3 Draw the outline in ink or waterproof marker.

4 Add details (clothing, hair, shoes, and face) to create your basic line drawing.

5 Now use very **diluted** black watercolor to create a light gray color for where the shadows are. The light is mostly catching his face, chest, and hips on the left, since that's where he's holding the sparkler. Most of his right side and his feet are in shadow, and the arm holding the sparkler is in shadow because it's facing toward his body, not the light. Finally, add a tiny bit more black to the diluted gray, and darken the areas farthest from the light—the back of his head, right shoulder, elbow, and leg.

Now that we've tried one together, practice a few on your own. Remember, your figures don't need to be perfect. Have fun!

Adding a Face

Faces show thoughts, emotions, and attitudes. We all have noses, eyes, and mouths, but their different shapes, sizes, and placement help make faces unique.

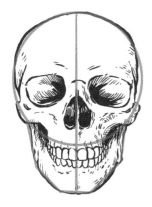 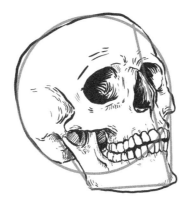 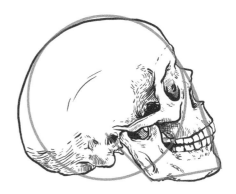

When drawing a head, start with a large circle and add triangular curved lines for the lower jaw. Then draw three lines in the center of the face. The top line, usually at the middle of the circle, hits the eyes and top of the ears. The middle line hits the nostrils and bottom of the earlobes, and the bottom line is where the mouth will be.

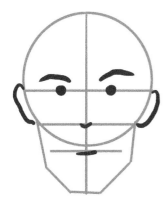 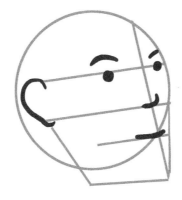 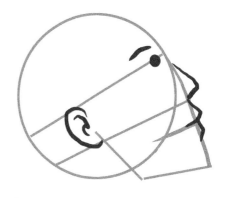

A good exercise is to create self-portraits using a mirror, sketching various expressions like smiling, crying, laughing, or screaming.

  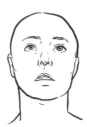 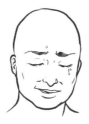 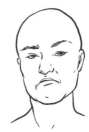 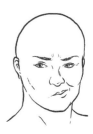

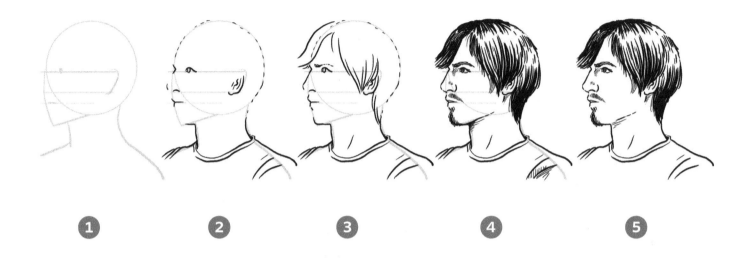

1   Draw the head in profile (side view), with a circle for the head and a triangle for the jaw. Then draw the three lines where the features will be.

2   Try drawing the features first, then the head shape. Draw the upper eyelid and eye, then the nostril, and finally a curved dash for the tip of the nose. The lips meet like a sideways V (>) and usually are the same length as the nostril. Add the ear.

3   Now connect the forehead to the nose, and lips to chin. Add an indent at the eyes and between the chin and mouth. Add some hair strands, too.

4   Add thick strokes for the hair and some dashes or stippling for facial hair. Do a bit of shading near the eyes and under the chin.

5   Finish the figure by erasing the sketch lines.

Now that we've tried one together, practice a few on your own. Remember, your figures don't need to be perfect. Have fun!

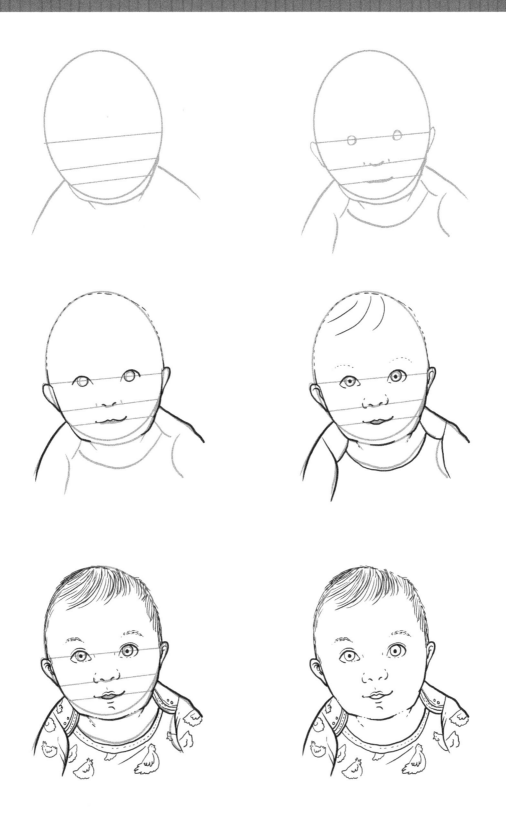

Making a Scene

WORDS TO LEARN

foreground: the very front of a scene, closest to the viewer

middleground: the space between the foreground and background

background: the farthest part of a scene

composition: the arrangement of the things in your art

We can now use past lessons to make whole drawings. Using the Movement activity (page 28), we can show figures relating to one another. We can place them close together or at a distance using perspective (page 36). We can also use shading (page 44) to suggest time of day or create a mood.

The **foreground**, where a lot of main storytelling happens, contains the finest details. The **middleground** often shows where the scene takes place and has secondary figures. The **background** shows setting and holds less detail.

Composition is how we arrange a scene. You can start by drawing a shape or letter and putting all the important subjects and details inside. Outside the shape will be the setting, small details, and muted colors.

1.   Start with a stick figure. For this exercise, we'll draw a woman at the beach.

2.   Use short dashes for the main body parts. She's in a skirt, so don't draw too much of the leg.

3.   Fill in the basic shapes of the body, then outline the dress. Add some waves.

4.   Draw a basic outline of the figure and the dock she's leaning against. Finish with final lines and details.

5.   Time for shading! The light is coming from the right, as if she's watching a sunset, so try to have your shading show that.

TIP:

Artists often use a technique called atmospheric perspective. This creates an illusion of depth by showing distant objects as paler, less detailed, and usually a bit bluer.

Now that we've tried one together, practice a few on your own. Remember, your figures don't need to be perfect. Have fun!

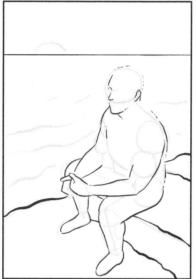

Photo Aid

The advantage of using a photograph to practice drawing is that you can always refer back to the photo, unlike a live subject, so there's no rush.

When taking a photo for reference, or using one you already have, think about your past lessons. Try taking a picture that shows movement. Avoid figures wearing all black or baggy clothing, because it can be hard to see their shape. Avoid cutting off the feet, arms, or half the head. Try taking the photograph in sunlight to get good highlights and shadows. Using flash can overexpose things.

Museums are great places to take photos for reference. They have wonderful collections of sculptures, armor, and taxidermied animals, beautifully lit and posed.

1   Start with a simple stick figure to capture the form.

2   Use basic shapes to finish and fill in the form.

3   Draw the simple lines of the figure
and its clothing.

4   Complete the details for the face, clothing, and patterns.

5   Finish the figure by removing the
sketch lines.

Now that we've tried one together, practice a few on your own. Remember, your figures don't need to be perfect. Have fun!

Statues are great to use because of their dramatic poses and lighting. Try practicing with this photo.

Photos with friends are fantastic to work from, too. Try practicing with this photo.

Street photography can result in something really dynamic. Try practicing with this photo.

In Your Home

First, you need a willing model, perhaps a family member or friend. Pick a well-lit spot so that you can see clearly and get interesting shadows. Try outdoors or inside near a window. Just make sure your subject is comfortable.

Begin with a stick figure, then sketch any surrounding setting you'd like. It's okay to start out messy, drawing quick planning lines and fuller lines. There's plenty of time later for final, detailed lines.

If your model is holding a difficult pose, set a timer. At 10-minute intervals, allow your model to stretch and drink some water. Use your model as a guide and have fun drawing what you see and imagine. Maybe your figure is fighting a dragon or exploring space! Remember, your figures don't need to be perfect.

Turn a friend into a superhero! Pose them in a way that shows off their superpower. Can they fly? Do they shoot lasers out of their eyes?

1

2

3

1   Position your model next to a window with plenty of daylight. Have fun dressing them up. Maybe you have a cape, a Halloween costume, or cool jewelry.

2   Sit close to them and start your quick sketch in light pencil. Sketch a hint of their costume and powers, too. Once you have the figure drawn out and you find yourself looking less and less at your model, let them take a break from posing. Continue drawing details, then add color. If there's something you're unsure of in your drawing, kindly ask your model to re-pose.

3   Add basic shapes to fill out and finish the sketch.

4   Now draw your major outlines with a black marker, pen, or colored pencil that doesn't smear when erased.

5   Erase your pencil sketch, and then finish up details and fine lines.

6   Now it's up to you. Color in your lines with marker, colored pencils, or crayon. Remember to show light and shadow!

Here are some other scenarios you can do at home using family and friends and objects around the house. Grab a timer and start with short sessions of 10 to 15 minutes. After a few drawings, increase the time to 20 minutes, then 30 minutes. Remember to have fun!

- Draw your parents while they cook.

- Have a sibling or friend pose in a Halloween costume and create a fantasy scene.

- Use a mirror and do a self-portrait.

- Have a friend pose as an explorer and draw them in a prehistoric world.

- Set up a scene with dolls and action figures, and light them.

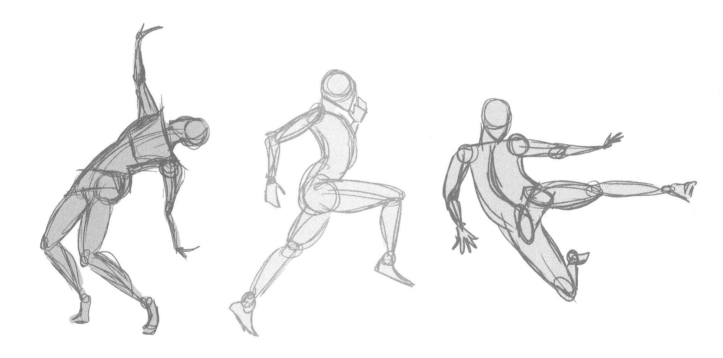

Out in the World

Let's draw outdoors! Take your parents to local parks, cafés, and festivals and sketch people going about their day. This exercise might be initially challenging because people aren't posing for you, but, again, don't stress about being perfect.

Work fast and loose in light pencil to capture your subject. You can do many sketches and add final lines and color later. If you draw someone who's sitting, drinking coffee, or reading, you'll probably have more time to sketch them. If you pick someone playing a sport, they might move too fast.

With your parents, try to visit your local park and find a picnic table to set up your workspace. Look for someone who may be reading or playing games on their phone. Find someone sitting because someone standing could move away at any minute.

1   Begin by drawing a quick stick figure in light pencil.

2   Add basic shapes to fill out the figure. Try adding a bit of setting in light pencil, too.

3   Sketch some details lightly, such as clothing, facial features, and hair. You can finish this sketch at home or continue to a final drawing if the person doesn't move from their pose.

4   With a marker or pen that doesn't smear, start drawing overall outlines of the figure, clothing, and some scenery.

5   Finish with finer line details, such as shading and textures. Add color if you have the time and supplies.

* When you go to a coffee shop or restaurant, sketch someone who's sitting. Once you finish, draw someone else in the café on the same piece of paper. Keep going until you have a whole scene.

* Visit the zoo and sketch people watching the animals. Try drawing similarities between the movements or expressions of the animals and those of the people observing them.

* Visit a museum and take inspiration from the art. You can find a drawing or painting you like and draw someone in that style.

TIP:

I keep a tote bag packed and ready to go. In it are pencils, an eraser, a sharpener, markers, a sketchbook (that can be used for watercolor, ink, and markers), and sometimes a watercolor palette with an Aqua Pen. Aqua Pens are paintbrushes filled with water, so you don't need a cup when using them. Try making your own bag of supplies.

Creating a Finished Illustration

Let's learn about creating a finished illustration from beginning to end. First, gather some supplies.

- Paper made for mixed media

- Pencil

- Eraser

- Ink: fine-line Sharpie, Pentel pocket brush, Micron pens, or Pentel Hybrid Technica in nib sizes 06 and 03 (for details)

- Colored pencils, if you're worried about smudging or bleeding

When creating a piece of art, I pick my reference from online or my own photograph. Then I lightly sketch everything in pencil, erasing unnecessary lines afterward.
    If I'm using wet media (like watercolors), I color first and then ink my final drawing.
    If I'm using dry media, I'll ink and *then* color.

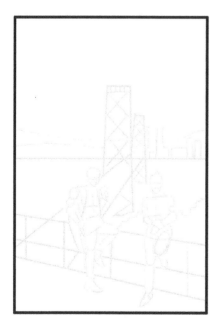

Come up with a story, then the characters and the setting. In this example, kids are enjoying a snow day.

1. Start with a light pencil sketch of each figure, from the stick skeleton to the basic shapes.

2. Add the main outline in your thickest marker, getting the most important bits, such as the shape of their clothes and the sled.

3 Finish the drawing by adding smaller details in a finer ink pen. This picture is going to be colored, so shade in the color step rather than **stipple** or **crosshatch**.

4 Erase the sketch lines. Use colored pencils to shade lightly, then slowly build up color by applying more pressure to make shadows.

Now let's use watercolor to illustrate kids picking flowers in a field. This picture has a triangular composition.

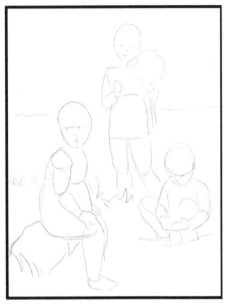  

1. Make a very light sketch using only a few simple lines, because once watercolor is on top, you won't be able to erase the lines. Draw basic shapes to create the figures, then erase the lines inside these shapes once you have your full form.

2. Add color. Start out with light washes of mostly water and a little watercolor.

3. Slowly build value with more paint. (With watercolor, less is more.) Let the picture dry.

4

5

4   Once it's dry, draw the final outline in pen or marker.

5   Add details. Then use colored pencils or colored marker to add pops of color on the lips, some flowers, and wherever else you feel could use more!

FURTHER READING

Learn more about figure drawing and get inspiration from some of my favorite books:

Figure Drawing for All It's Worth and *Drawing the Heads and Hands* by Andrew Loomis. The second one is a classic. My grandfather used it in high school!

Beginning Drawing Atelier by Juliette Aristides. This book presents relatively advanced lessons on drawing and shading. Each chapter tackles the basics of classical drawing.

Urban Watercolor Sketching by Felix Scheinberger. This book is filled with fun, great art and teaches you how to sketch fast and outside the studio.

The Fantasy Illustrator's Technique Book by Gary A. Lippincott. If you love fantasy like me and want to do more of that next, this book is fantastic!

Portrait Painting Atelier: Old Master Techniques and Contemporary Applications by Suzanne Brooker. Did you like drawing faces while doing the activities? Try this book to focus on drawing portraits and to learn more about using paint.

Imagine a Forest by Dinara Mirtalipova. If you enjoyed working on basic shapes or drawing patterns, this book is a great introduction to drawing in a less anatomical, more folk-art style.

Making an Impression by Geninne Zlatkis. If you love art and want to try a new medium, this book is filled with great how-to projects, such as how to make your own stamps.

Picture This: How Pictures Work by Molly Bang. This in-depth technical book explains what makes a good picture. It explores subjects such as composition, graphic design, and evoking emotion with linework.

Draw Your Day: An Inspiring Guide to Keeping a Sketch Journal by Samantha Dion Baker. I've been drawing every single day since I was a kid, so I have an attic full of sketchbooks. The key to becoming an artist is to keep practicing, and this book has exercises that keep you going when you get stuck.

INDEX

ABOUT THE AUTHOR

Angela Rizza graduated from the Fashion Institute of Technology in New York City in 2011 and since then has been creating artwork in Mahopac, New York. Her work is inspired by the wildlife around her home and her favorite childhood stories. She enjoys teaching art and creating activity books that help others learn and use their imagination.

CPSIA information can be obtained
at www.ICGtesting.com
Printed in the USA
JSHW030304150821
17810JS00002B/4

How to Draw

How to Draw

Easy Techniques and Step-by-Step Drawings

for Kids

Aaria Baid

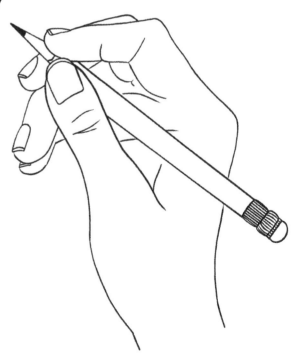

ROCKRIDGE
PRESS

For general information on our other products and services or to obtain technical support, please contact our Customer Care Department within the United States at (866) 744-2665 or outside the U.S. at (510) 253-0500.

Rockridge Press publishes its books in a variety of electronic and print formats. Some content that appears in print may not be available in electronic books, and vice versa.

Interior and Cover Designer: William Mack
Production Editor: Erum Khan

ISBN: Print 978-1-64152-181-9 | eBook 978-1-64611-100-8

I dedicate this book
to anyone who has
ever been inspired
to draw after seeing
my art!

Contents

Introduction

Hi there! If you've picked up this book, chances are you like to draw. Drawing is something we've all tried—whether we doodled something in school when we were bored, or we may have even attended art classes or a workshop.

A common misconception is that drawing is a talent given to a select few. The truth is that anyone can learn to draw. All you have to do is get started, gain some knowledge about the basic skills needed, and practice as you explore different topics and themes. And did I mention that drawing is supposed to be fun?

The Five Ps of Becoming an Artist

Let's begin with the assumption that you want to improve your drawing skills. You think, "I'm going to practice regularly now." So you draw something every day. Some days you like your creations; some days you don't. Yet you keep drawing.

Then, one fine day, you look at what you've drawn and realize, "Wow. I *have* improved!" You compare your current drawings to your old ones and think, "This is just like magic!"

Now drawing seems exciting. You've learned the secret. The secret to becoming an artist is summed up in one word: PRACTICE. Good old slow and steady practice. Now you may be thinking, "Oh, so all I have to do is practice forever?"

Yes and no. Practice is made better with PLAY. Play with art! Draw things that are fun to draw. Draw things that put you in a good mood. Draw things that are easy for you to draw.

Next, after you practice and play with art, also have fun with the PROCESS. Ask yourself, "When am I in the mood to draw?" Maybe you like to draw in the evenings or when you're free after lunch. Trust the process and you'll find inspiration when you least expect it.

Now, if you're *practicing* and *playing* with the *process*, lightly keep track of your PROGRESS. Keep your sketches in a separate file or sketchbook, and whenever you feel inclined, see your improvement—which brings us to the fifth P: PRAISE! Praise yourself and celebrate your improvement. Cheer yourself on and give yourself a pat on the back for every victory, no matter how big or small.

So, there you have it: Practice. Play. Process. Progress. Praise. Those are all you need to be an artist—and that's where this book comes in.

Part 1 of this book gives you the basics to start your practice: drawing terms, techniques, and plenty of exercises for warming up.

Part 2 of this book has plenty of fun drawing projects for you to play with and discover your own interests in the creative process.

What You Need to Get Started

All the activities in the book require only a pencil and an eraser. For the step-by-step drawings, I recommend that you draw the guidelines lightly so they can be easily erased and then the final drawing can be defined with darker pencil lines.

I believe that you can be a brilliant artist who, most importantly, enjoys the process and finds joy in seeing your constant improvement.

Let's get started!

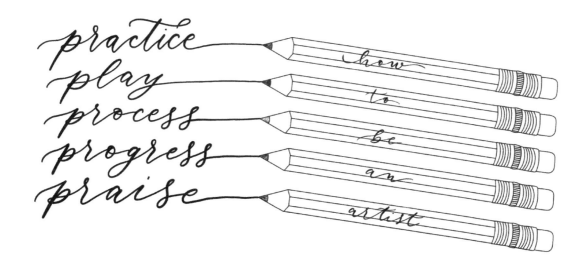

PART ONE
Art School

THE TOOL KIT
Lines and Shapes

BASIC PRINCIPLES OF DRAWING

Let's get acquainted with these basic principles. A little bit of art theory is always good to know!

1. **Mass:** When drawing anything, there's one very basic concept: **mass**. Mass is a shapeless space of any size. Mass is the foundation of your drawing.

2. **Shapes:** The next step is finding the **shapes** in the mass. At this point, the shapes are free-flowing and can be changed.

3. **Form:** You can add lines to create **form**. Form is when you refine the basic shapes.

4. **Detail:** Add more shapes and lines to create **detail**. Detail includes all the finer aspects—darkness, texture, etc.

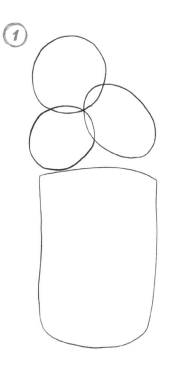

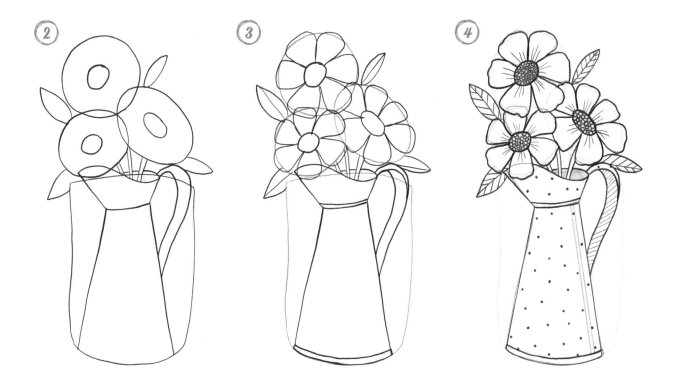

BASIC TYPES OF LINES

│	Vertical line	· · · · · · ·	Dotted line	∿	S-curve
────	Horizontal line	⌇	Random line	WW	Fine zigzag
⌒	Curved line	╱	Right slant line	- - - - -	Hyphenated line
◠◠◠	Zigzag	╲	Left slant line	◡◡◡	Scalloped line

Practice Patterns with Lines:

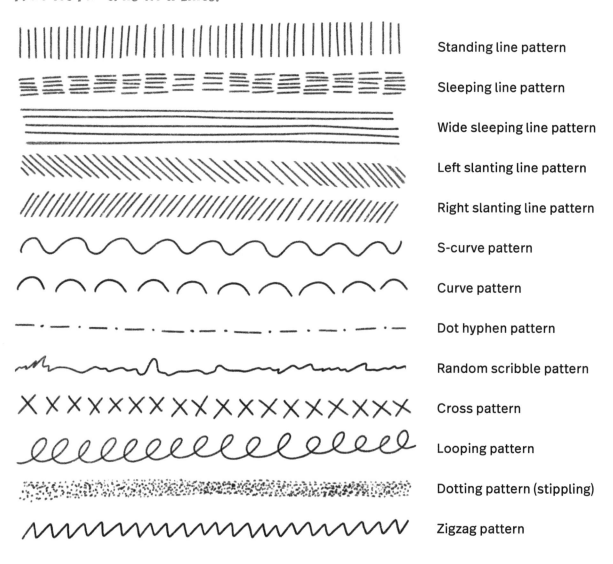

Standing line pattern

Sleeping line pattern

Wide sleeping line pattern

Left slanting line pattern

Right slanting line pattern

S-curve pattern

Curve pattern

Dot hyphen pattern

Random scribble pattern

Cross pattern

Looping pattern

Dotting pattern (stippling)

Zigzag pattern

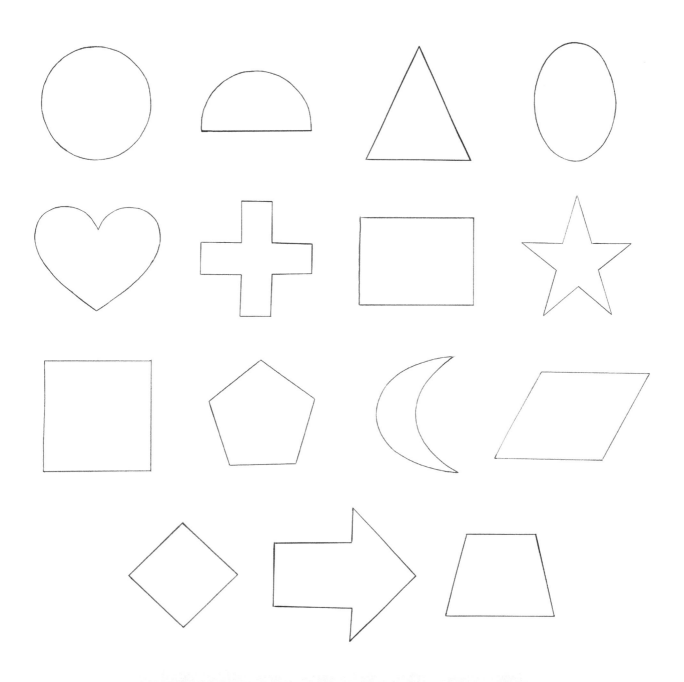

ARTIST TIP Practice drawing shapes freehand to increase confidence. Shapes are used to create the subject or object being drawn. They are made of curves and/or lines. You can combine shapes to create complex structures and make up your own shapes as well.

DRAW A HOUSE USING BASIC SHAPES

A house is a very versatile structure. You can create it with lines, curves, and textures. Here's a basic example:

1. Start with the basic shapes.

2. Add a chimney and roof edge.

3. Draw lines on the roof.

4. Add textures as indicated.

5. Add windows and a door.

6. Shade lightly and draw more components.

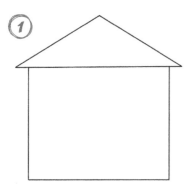

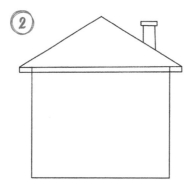

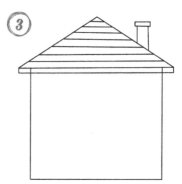

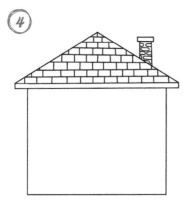

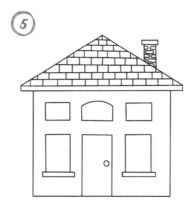

ARTIST TIP You can depict houses in many ways. Here are some examples to get you inspired:

A house is basically constructed with shapes; the more shapes and lines you use, the more complex it seems. But it's easier than you think: All you have to do is create the basic shape first and build up the details within that. You can find out more about this in activity 13 (page 80).

Detailed house

Silhouette house with trees in the background

Treehouse

DRAW A PIZZA SLICE

Pizza is really fun to draw (and eat!). It's shaped like a circle, and we eat it in triangles.

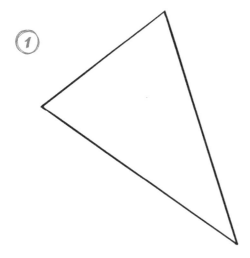

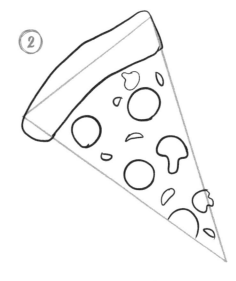

1. Start by drawing a triangle (tilted or straight).

2. Draw shapes for the toppings (circles, mushroom shapes, small random ones—anything!) and a blunt-edged rectangle for the crust.

3. Add a scribble line around the triangle, with some drips for melting cheese.

4. Finish by erasing the triangle outline, and add texture to the pizza with straight lines and random lines.

DRAW A DONUT

Who doesn't love to draw (and eat) donuts? Donuts are simple to draw, and you can create new designs—each donut can be an original masterpiece.

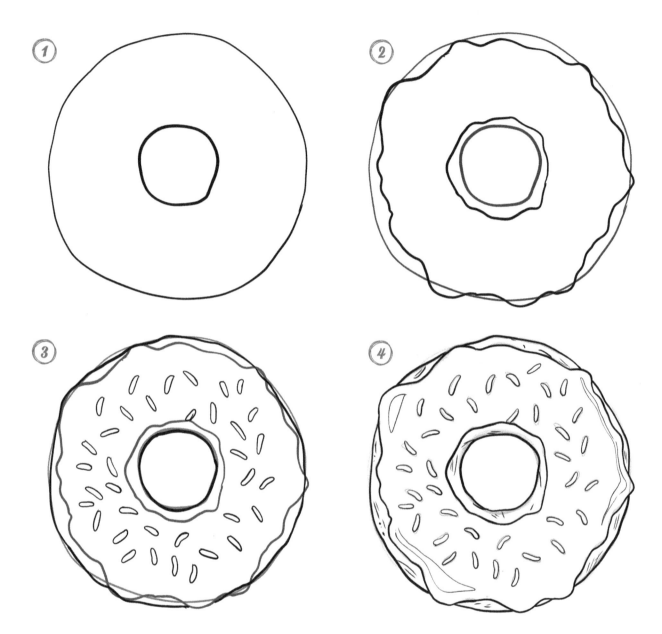

1. Draw a circle and a smaller one in the center.

2. Draw similar-size circles in a scribble style.

3. Add a rough outline to the biggest circle and add sprinkles.

4. Erase the guidelines and add highlights and textures.

DRAW A CUPCAKE

You can create so many styles just by playing around with different shapes and decorations.

1. Draw a triangle and an oval.

2. Extend two lines downward and join them with a curved line.

3. Add curves on the triangle and vertical lines for a cupcake paper on the bottom.

4. Join the top lines with curves and add a scalloped border to the paper cup below.

5. Add more lines and dots for decoration, and customize with a cherry, bunting, chocolate sticks, etc.

6. Add texture to the cake rim and erase the guidelines.

2

3D Shapes

BASIC PRINCIPLES OF DRAWING 3D SHAPES

A **2D shape** has length (x) and height (y). It looks flat on the paper. A **3D shape** has length (x), height (y), and also depth (z). Depth is created by adding lines and shading. You can use 3D shapes to create more realistic drawings.

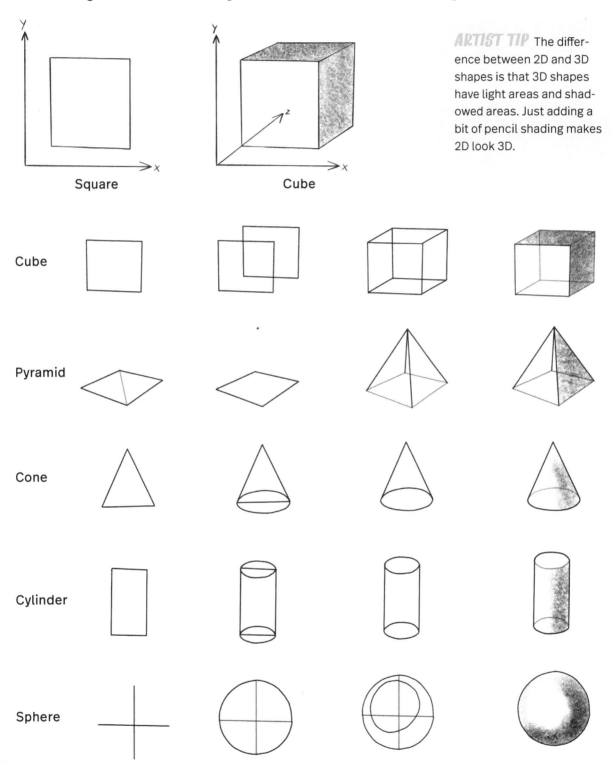

ARTIST TIP The difference between 2D and 3D shapes is that 3D shapes have light areas and shadowed areas. Just adding a bit of pencil shading makes 2D look 3D.

Square

Cube

Cube

Pyramid

Cone

Cylinder

Sphere

DRAW SPORTY SPHERES

A single sphere can become a whole variety of sports balls. Start with a circle, add lines, and use your pencil to darken areas for a 3D look.

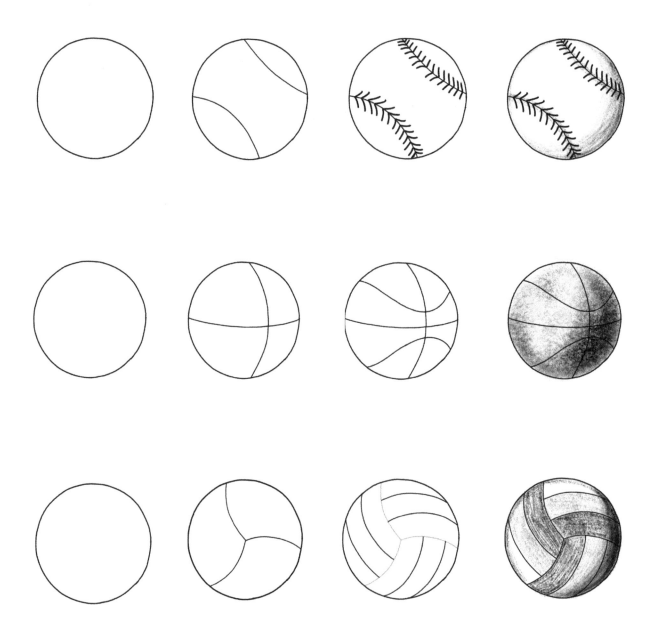

ARTIST TIP Other sporty drawing ideas with the same sphere are a tennis ball, soccer ball, bowling ball, or golf ball.

DRAW A RUBIK'S CUBE

The Rubik's Cube remains the best-selling puzzle toy of all time. Knowing how to draw a cube will come in handy for all sorts of drawings.

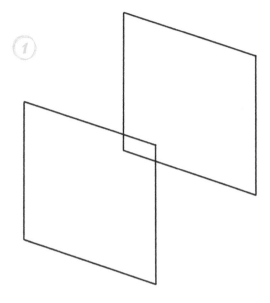

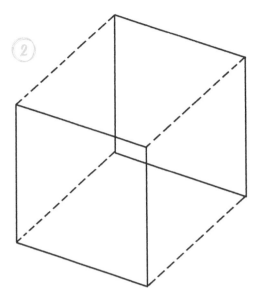

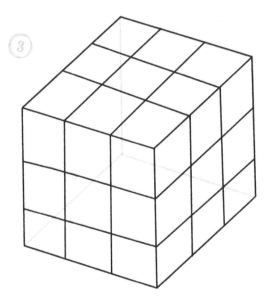

1. Draw two parallelograms (like a slanted square) and make them intersect to form a small rectangle.

2. Join the lines to form a cube. You can see three surfaces now.

3. Roughly divide each surface into nine squares by drawing four lines— two vertical and two horizontal.

4. Erase the guidelines, shade along the lines, and add a dot on each intersection.

DRAW AN ICE CREAM CONE

An ice cream cone is a cone shape and circles. You can make it a single-, double-, triple- . . . or even a 10-scoop cone!

1. Draw an upside-down cone.

2. Add three ovals (scoops) on top and crisscross lines on the cone.

3. Draw a random scribble around the scoops and double the crisscross lines.

4. Add details, like drizzle, dots, lines, a cherry, etc.

5. Draw little squares between the criss-cross lines.

6. Erase the guidelines.

7. Use your pencil to add texture and shading for the 3D effect.

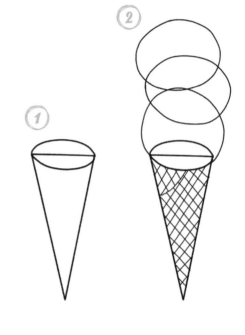

DRAW A CAKE

It's almost as satisfying to draw a cake as it is to eat one. Okay, not really, but now you can make great birthday cards.

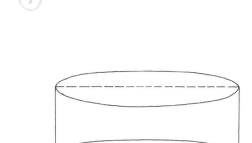
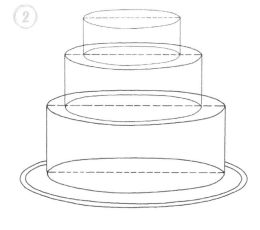

1. Start by drawing a wide cylinder (a rectangle with ovals on top and bottom).

2. Add smaller cylinders on top. Add a cake plate, too.

3. Add icing, candles, lines, dots, etc. Make the plate fancy with some curved legs.

4. Erase the guidelines and use your pencil to "color" in your drawing. Add some more details, like flickering candles, shadows on the surface, etc.

DARK AND LIGHT
Shading

BASIC PRINCIPLES OF SHADING

Shading is like "painting" with a pencil. You have to imagine the color values in tones of black and white. But unlike a paintbrush, a pencil is easier to maneuver. Shading enhances your art by turning flat 2D shapes into 3D on the paper.

Shading also leads you to experiment with the range of graphite tones and textures in your pencil. Pencils come in different grades: HB, 2B, 3B . . . all the way up to 10B. You also find 2H, 3H, and F grades. Simply put: H = hard, B = black, F = fine. The greater the number next to the H/B/F, the harder/darker/finer it is. B pencils are great for shading. H pencils are better suited for drawing.

A single pencil can give you a range of tones just by varying the pressure you put on it. Light pressure creates sheer, fine strokes. Hard pencil pressure creates dark, strong lines and textures.

ARTIST TIP

Artists use a variety of pencils. A good combination to get started with is HB for drawing and 6B for shading. You can incorporate other pencil grades into your work as you get comfortable.

Range of tones from light to dark

Textures using the pencil tip and edge of pencil

Another important aspect of shading is **blending**. You can blend the graphite by using the following tools to achieve a soft, dreamy look.

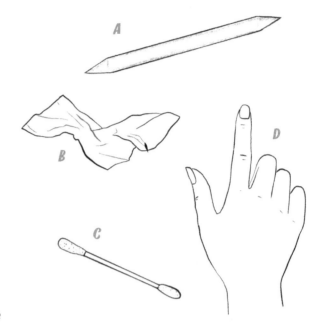

A. **Blending stump/tortillon:** This is a rolled-up paper you can use to smudge graphite. You can buy it at most art stores, but don't worry if you don't have one, because there are household items you can use instead.

B. **Tissue paper:** You can roll up tissue paper to form a point or use it flat to blend. It offers interesting textures, depending on how soft or rough it is.

C. **Cotton swab/Q-tip:** This will provide a softer finish than a blending stump.

D. **Fingers:** No tools? No problem! Just use your fingers. All the great artists have done it, and it's fun—like finger painting.

How to Blend

1. Draw your pencil textures.

2. Use your blending tool of choice to smudge them.

3. Remember, you can keep adding pencil textures over this and then blending in layers until you feel that it looks just right.

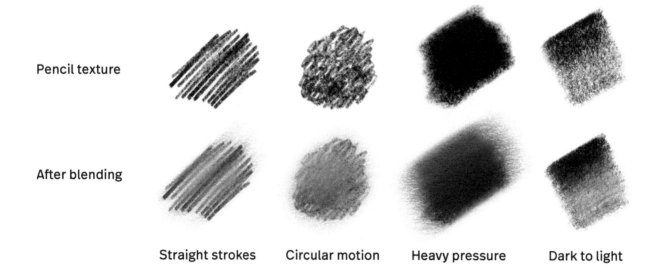

Pencil texture

After blending

Straight strokes   Circular motion   Heavy pressure   Dark to light

FRUITS

Fruits are great for drawing since you can find them at home and use them directly as a reference; they are also very helpful when you practice shading. They have highlights, lighter and darker areas, and plenty of textures to keep you interested.

1. Draw the basic outline.

2. Add details, including areas to be left white.

3. Shade with pencil and add more details.

Apples can have a cute leaf on the stem and highlights to indicate their roundness.

Each grape is a work of art in its own right. Each one has a small highlight and the grape leaf is prominent with deep veins. Shade the leaf edges dark.

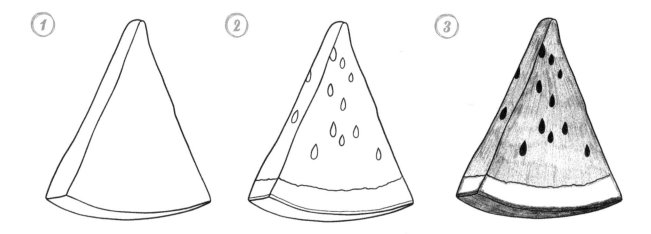

A watermelon slice has many tones: medium for the top, white for the next layer, and dark gray at the bottom. Remember, when shading you have to imagine colors in tones of black, white, and gray, depending on how light or dark they are.

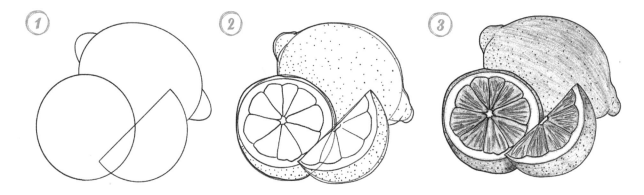

Lemons have cool textures: dots on the surface and wavy lines on the inside.

DRAW (AND SHADE) A COCONUT TREE

Coconut trees are great for practicing lines. You can draw these very easily and use them in landscapes.

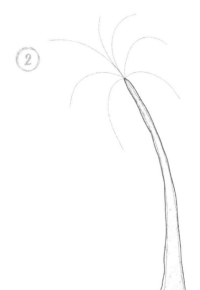

ARTIST TIP
Palm trees are similar to coconut trees; some just have straight, bigger trunks.

1. Draw a basic outline.

2. Draw a random outline around the trunk and shade lightly.

3. Add small lines on each leaf line to create the spreading leaves. Draw lines on the trunk.

4. Add details: coconuts, grass, and pencil textures.

DRAW (AND SHADE) A FLOWER

Flowers are pleasing things to draw. They are packed with tiny details, soft contrasts, and symmetrical perfection.

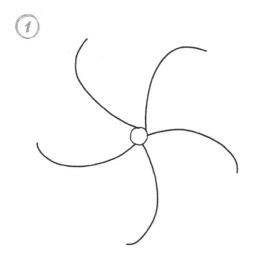

1. Draw a circle and five curving lines.

2. Using the curving lines, draw the petals (make the edges a little uneven to look natural).

3. Shade the inner part of the petals dark and the rest lighter.

4. Blend the shading and add some pencil lines on top for depth.

DRAW (AND SHADE) WATER DROPLETS

To draw water droplets, you just need to understand where the shadows fall. On a transparent object, the shadow falls on the same side as the light source. It's the opposite with a solid object.

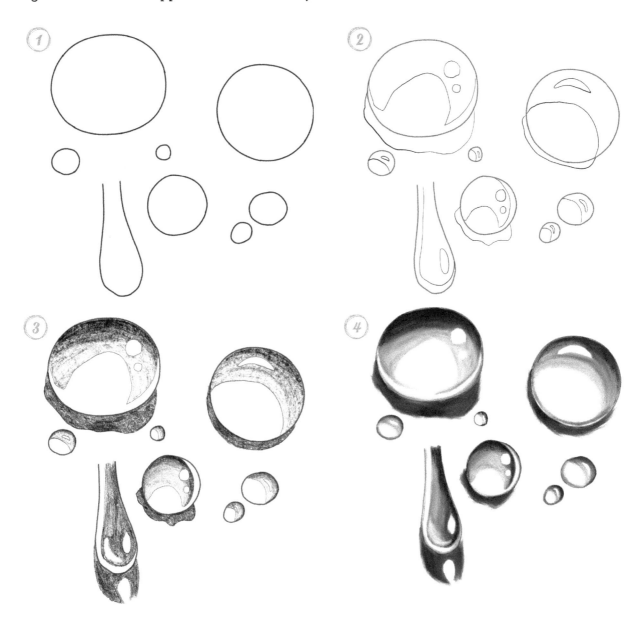

1. Draw basic outlines for the droplets, which can be different sizes.

2. Add areas to be shaded, and within them, draw small highlights to be left white.

3. Shade the areas from dark to light (choose a direction and try to be consistent). The big droplets have a shadow that is entirely dark.

4. Blend the shapes and layer pencil on them until you get a glassy finish.

POP OUT OF THE PAGE
Foreshortening

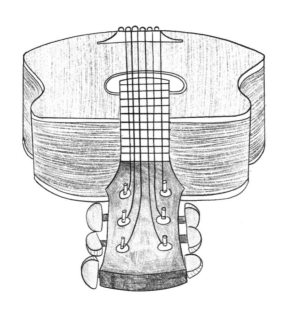

BASIC PRINCIPLES OF FORESHORTENING

Foreshortening is drawing an object so it looks compressed or enlarged. Hold your hand in front of you and change its direction. See how when it's directly in front, it looks flat, and when you're turning it sideways, it becomes thinner and the fingers line up behind each other? Foreshortening is a way of drawing these different angles and perspectives.

It is something of an optical illusion. Look at this example:

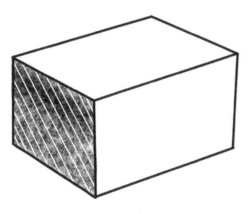

This box, which is farther away, has a smaller width (the shaded bit) and relatively longer length.

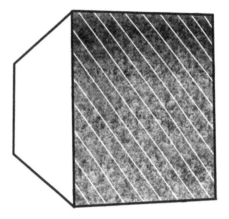

The same box, when facing the viewer and nearer, gives us a larger **close-up**. The length matters less.

Foreshortening Tips

A long object (like this drinking straw) can be reduced to a much smaller size when looking at it straight and not sideways.

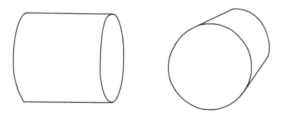

The more foreshortening you do, the more circular the end of the object is.

WAYS OF FORESHORTENING BOOKS

Books may have a simple structure—rectangles with pages in between—yet there are lots of angles when they're positioned differently.

This is how a book looks when it's perfectly straight in front of your eyes:

For all three rows:

1. Draw an outline.

2. Add lines to define the drawing.

3. Erase the outline and add shading and lines.

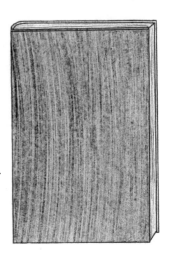

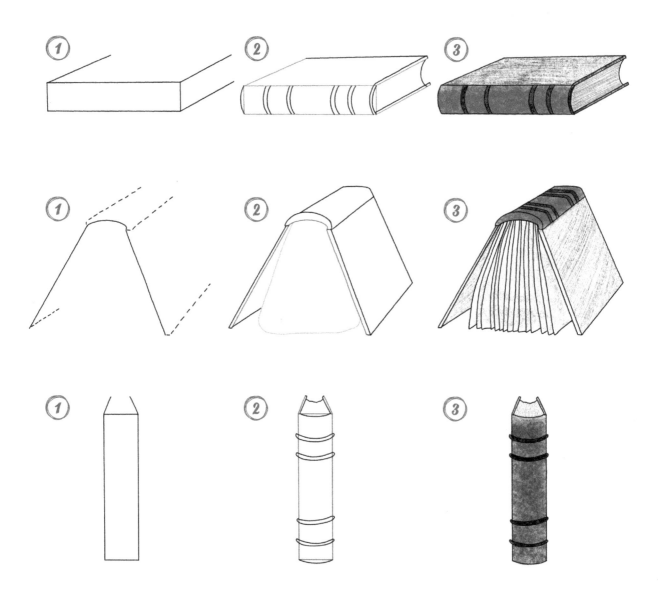

DRAW A GUITAR

Guitars are a great way to practice foreshortening, because they have many elements that look different when seen from various angles.

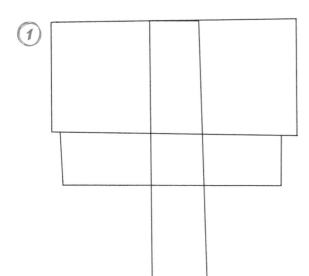

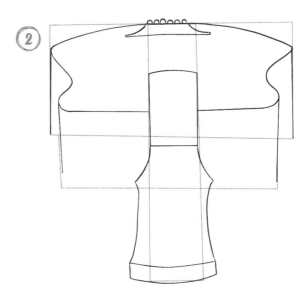

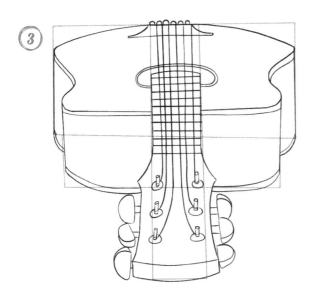

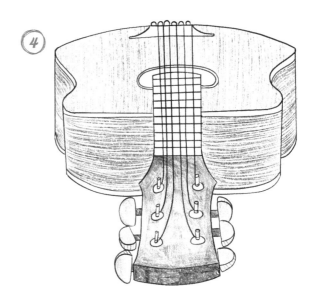

1. Make a base sketch with rectangles.

2. Add curves and vertical lines for the body. Draw the neck of the guitar.

3. Add details, like the strings, fretboard, and tuning pegs.

4. Erase the guidelines and add pencil shading. Done!

DRAW SNEAKERS

Do you prefer shoelaces or Velcro? Try out some shoelaces on high-top sneakers, because shoelaces are more challenging to draw. Challenges make drawing fun, right?

1. Draw a trapezoid.

2. Divide the trapezoid into thirds and draw a rough shoe shape over it.

3. Add details, like circles and the base of the sneaker, and draw lines for the shoelaces.

4. Double the shoelace lines (see how they overlap?), add a bow, and add pencil shading.

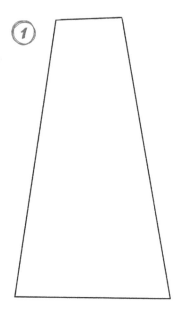

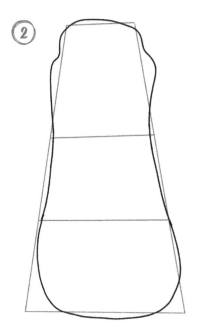

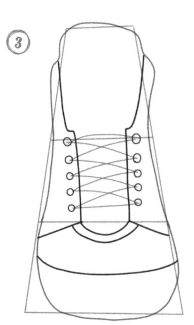

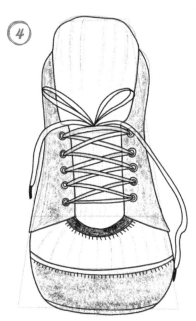

DRAW A CUP OF COFFEE

This cup of coffee is seen from an overhead position.

1. Draw two circles. The inner one is slightly off-center.

2. Add a rim and base on the cup, and a handle. Define the lines.

3. Add a design inside the coffee cup, including extra elements for the milk foam.

4. Use your pencil to add dark tones. Coffee is dark and the cup, saucer, and milk bubbles are white, so you see a big contrast. Blend the pencil texture and use your eraser to make white highlights and bubbles on the coffee.

Positive and Negative Space

BASIC PRINCIPLES OF POSITIVE AND NEGATIVE SPACE

Positive space is the object in focus, while **negative space** refers to the space that surrounds it. Negative space is a very cool aspect of drawing, because you're not actually thinking about the object—all you do is color around it, and it magically appears!

Here's a popular example of positive and negative space. What do you see first: the vase or the two faces? In the first image, the vase is black and the faces are white. In the second image, it's the opposite. People often think that the white is the positive space and the black is the negative, but the colors are irrelevant. The positive space is what you're focusing on.

Negative space is just as important as positive space. Some real-life examples are patterns on solid colors (e.g., curtains), shadows on windows, your own shadow on the sidewalk, and silhouettes.

DRAW A CHAIR

This will show you how a simple line drawing can be transformed into two studies of positive and negative space by reversing the colors. You can try this with any object.

1. Draw a chair. Don't worry about it being perfect.

2. To make the positive space black, shade the chair shape with your pencil.

3. To make the positive space white, shade around the chair, leaving the chair untouched. Erase the guidelines.

NEGATIVE LAYERING WITH TREES

Negative space and positive space are not only black and white.
There are many layers and colors that fall in between.

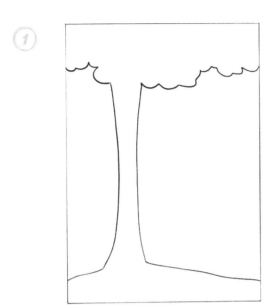

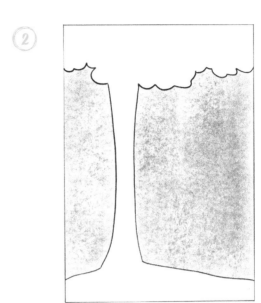

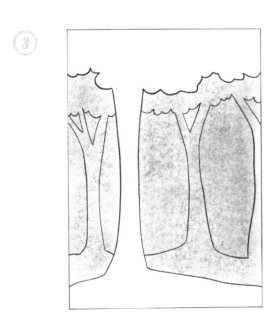

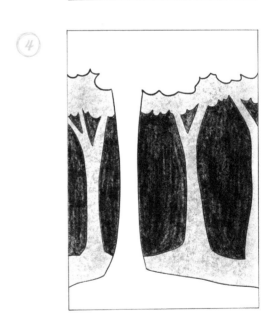

1. Draw a tree outline and a base (the ground). This is the first layer of positive space.

2. Shade the background lightly with your pencil. This is the first layer of negative space.

3. Draw more trees behind the first.

4. Shade the gaps behind these trees darker. See the three shades?

NEGATIVE SILHOUETTES WITH BIRDS ON A WIRE

Silhouettes are a quick and easy way to understand space and tones. You can create silhouettes with any object. Let's try silhouettes with these birds.

1. **Draw a rectangle and divide it into thirds. Add a basic bird outline to each space and have them all perched on a wire.**

2. **Now, in each space, make either the bird or the space lighter or darker. You can use different shades to create an interesting composition. Erase the guidelines.**

DOUBLE-EXPOSURE BEAR

Double exposure is an illusion achieved by using negative and positive space. It's a technique used in photography but is equally interesting in drawing. Try this double-exposure bear with a cool mountain vibe.

1. Draw a bear outline.

2. Add a series of pine trees (they can be different sizes and heights).

3. Color the pine trees with your pencil to make a silhouette effect. Add mountains with some ridges behind the trees.

4. Shade the sky lightly and add a moon and stars. Define the drawing with more shading. Your double-exposure bear is ready!

ARTIST TIP You can combine many landscapes with objects. Some examples are a beach scene in a seashell, an autumn landscape in a leaf, and a night sky in a deer silhouette.

BALANCING ACT
Proportion and Scale

BASIC PRINCIPLES OF PROPORTION AND SCALE

Although **proportion** is one of the finer aspects of drawing, all it means is the size of objects in relation to each other. It's not as hard as it sounds: You just need a little common sense, observation, and practice. Here's a comparison to illustrate the point:

You can draw things out of proportion to create an effect. Many famous painters, such as Pablo Picasso with his exaggerated faces and Salvador Dalí with his melting clocks, warped proportion.

Here's a quick example of how switching the proportions of the face, eyes, nose, and lips can create a big contrast. The first drawing is more realistic, while the second looks like a cartoon alien. Don't be afraid to play around with proportion; you can come up with really interesting variations.

WHAT IS SCALE?

Scale is making a drawing's dimensions (length, width, etc.) proportional to the original object. To do this, we use a ratio. This is helpful when we want to draw something accurately but it's way too big to fit on the paper, or when we want to make a small object appear larger. A simple example is this paper clip: The first one is the original size (ratio of 1:1), the second one is half the size (1:2), and the third one is double the size (2:1).

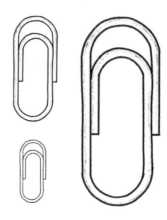

Proportion and Scale Techniques

These two techniques can help you get a good understanding of proportion and scale.

Grid method: You draw a grid over a reference image, which breaks down a complex shape into smaller squares. Then you just focus on drawing each square, and in no time you have the full image.

Measuring: You can use your hand, pencil, ruler, etc., to roughly measure and mark the distance of objects. This method is helpful for both reference and observation drawing.

6

DRAW AN EYE USING THE GRID METHOD

This method can help you draw any image, easy or difficult. The trick is to forget about the object. Once you divide the reference image, you just see the lines and curves in each square, and draw them, one by one.

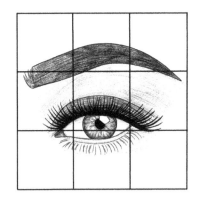

We already have a grid over the reference image (eye), so for this tutorial, just draw the same 9-square grid on your paper. Choose a square and start drawing exactly what you see. Don't think about it being an eye. Just focus on each square and draw only what you see there.

Erase the guidelines and shade the drawing.

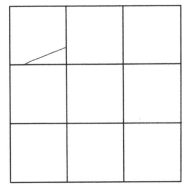
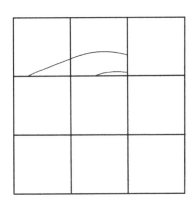
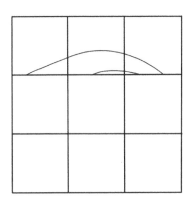

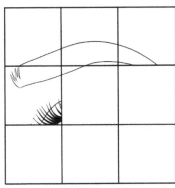
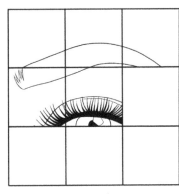
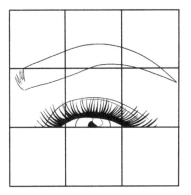

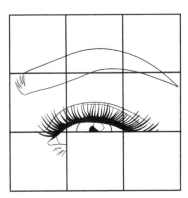
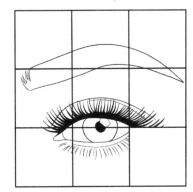
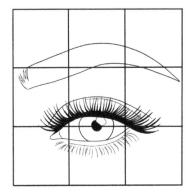

DRAW A BUTTERFLY USING THE GRID METHOD

Use the same grid technique to make a complex butterfly. It's easy as pie.

ARTIST TIP When using a grid, it's often easier to start in the center to keep the image balanced. Starting at the corners can sometimes warp your perception.

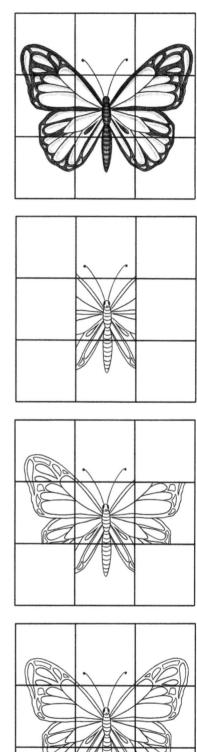

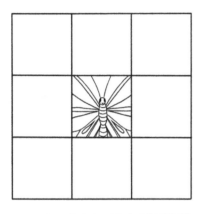

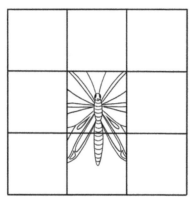

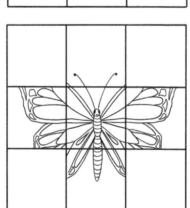

DRAW A FRUIT BASKET USING THE GRID METHOD

When it comes to multiple objects—in this case, lots of fruit—all those overlapping elements can seem confusing. Don't worry. Just focus on one fruit at a time, one line at a time.

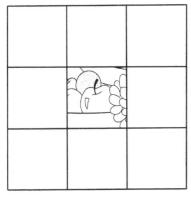

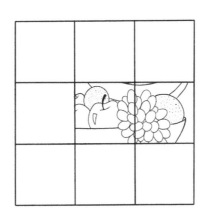

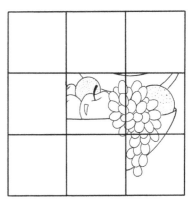

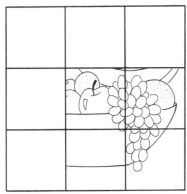

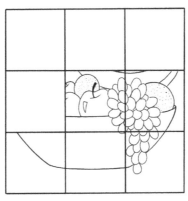

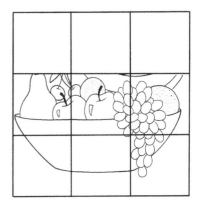

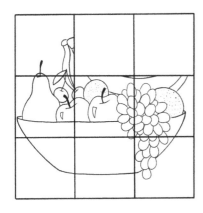

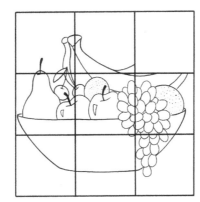

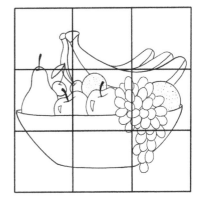

THE LONG ROAD AHEAD
One-Point Perspective

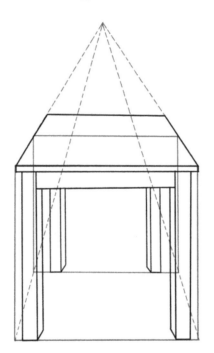

BASIC PRINCIPLES OF ONE-POINT PERSPECTIVE

Drawing using perspective is a way to make things look closer or farther away. There are three types: **one-point perspective**, **two-point perspective**, and **three-point perspective**. We'll discuss the first two.

A drawing has one-point perspective when it contains only one **vanishing point** (VP) on the horizon. One-point perspective is usually used for roads, railway tracks, etc. The lines converge at the VP.

Take a look at the image: The VP is placed on the main line (horizon). Lines from the VP extending in different directions are used to place objects on, above, or below the horizon.

You can use this guide to plot your drawings:

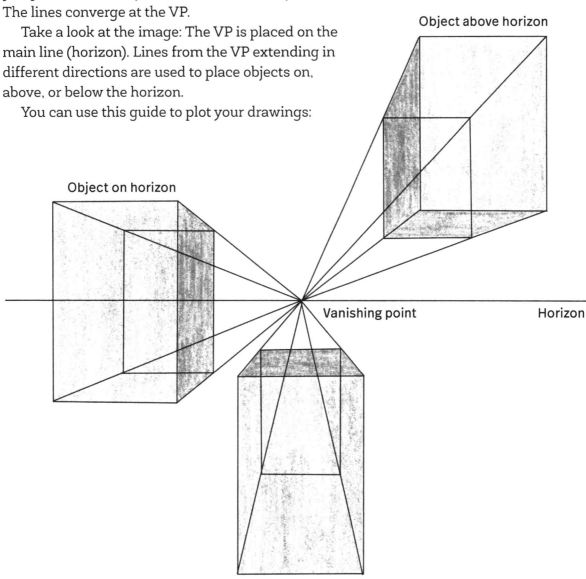

Object above horizon

Object on horizon

Vanishing point   Horizon

Object below horizon

ONE-POINT PERSPECTIVE: RAILWAY TRACKS

Let's use railway tracks as the central theme, with supporting elements on the sides.

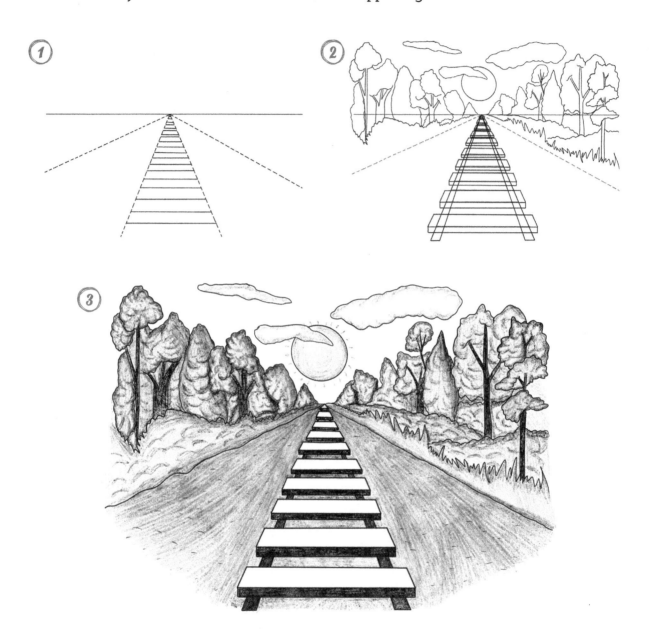

1. Draw a horizontal line (horizon) and place a dot on it (VP) in the center. From this point, two straight lines diverge (move away from each other) to form the tracks, and two more to form the road.

2. Add details on the tracks, and add trees on either side. Draw a sun and clouds.

3. Shade lightly and erase the guidelines. Now you know how to use one-point perspective!

ONE-POINT PERSPECTIVE: SMALL OBJECTS

Drawing relatively small objects (not buildings, bridges, etc.) gives you the freedom to focus on the details. Here's a table for you to practice.

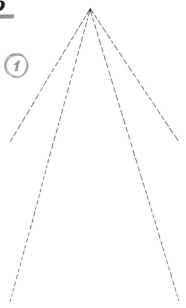

1. Draw the VP near the top of the paper, two long lines diverging from it, and a pair of shorter lines on the outside.

2. Use these guidelines to draw squares. A cubic structure appears.

3. Using the guidelines, add a tabletop and four legs.

4. Erase the guidelines to reveal the final result.

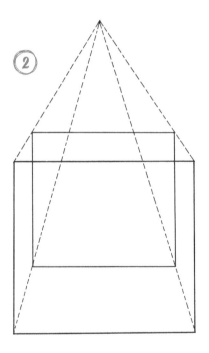

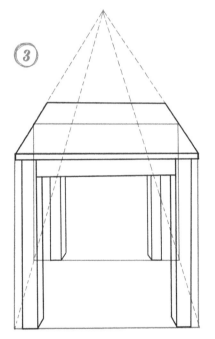

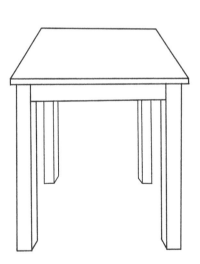

ONE-POINT PERSPECTIVE: LARGE OBJECTS

Large objects (e.g., airplanes, buildings, bridges) usually have to balance detail with their surroundings. This bridge has many elements to it (railings, walkway, etc.) and there's also the background of the cityscape.

1. Draw a horizon line with a VP. Draw two diverging lines (a triangle effect) for the bridge body.

2. Add the railings and the upper parts of the bridge. Notice how it becomes thinner and taller as it gets farther away.

3. Add lines for the railings and supports.

4. Shade for contrast and draw a cityscape on the horizon. Add clouds and shade the water lightly.

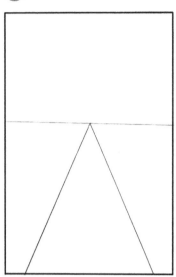

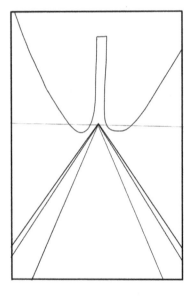

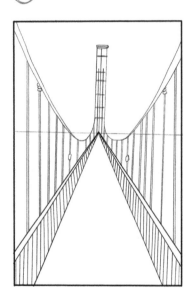

ONE-POINT PERSPECTIVE: ROAD WITH PALM TREES

Give this palm tree–lined road and gorgeous sunset a try.

1. Start by drawing a horizon. Add the road, its centerline markings, and its edges.

2. Add palm trees, which get smaller the nearer they are to the horizon.

3. Pencil in the leafy details; add clouds and a sun.

4. Emphasize the details with shading.

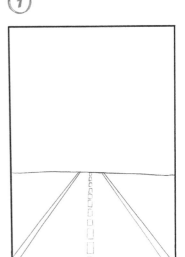

SEEING BOTH SIDES

Two-Point Perspective

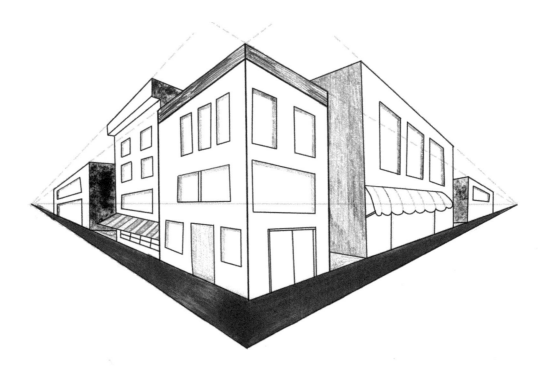

BASIC PRINCIPLES OF TWO-POINT PERSPECTIVE

One-point perspective focuses on only one side of an object, while two-point perspective requires seeing two sides. Two-point perspective has two vanishing points (VPs) on the horizon. In one-point perspective, the object becomes smaller as it nears the one VP, but in two-point perspective, the object is at an angle with our line of vision. The greater the angle created by the two sides, the closer the object is to the two vanishing points.

With two VPs, you get to draw multiple facets (sides) of the shape. Two-point perspective is used widely for architectural drawings, technical drawings, and for interior design.

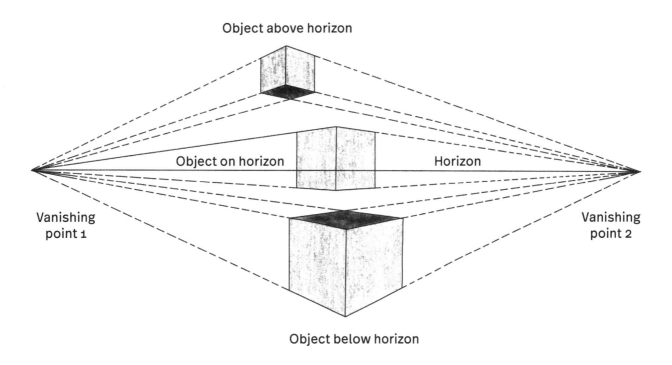

Object above horizon

Object on horizon   Horizon

Vanishing point 1

Vanishing point 2

Object below horizon

TWO-POINT PERSPECTIVE: TABLE AND VASE

Let's start with a simple table and vase. Since the vase is upright on the table, we don't need to worry about its perspective. We only need to use the lines for the table.

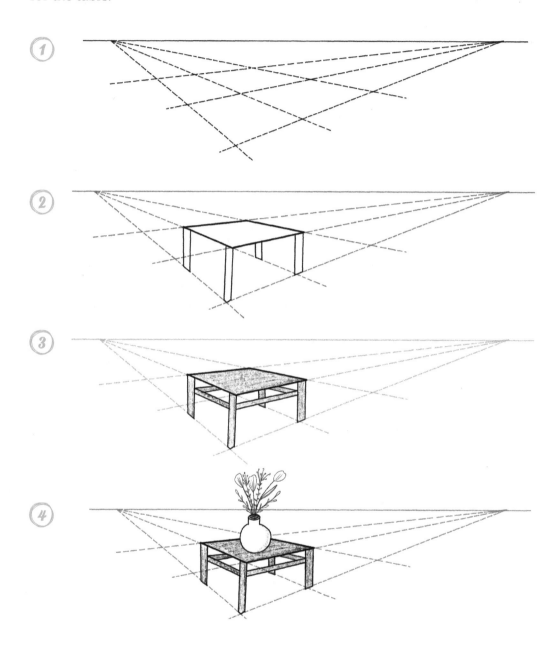

1. Start with drawing the horizon and three lines from each VP that meet to form a space for the table.

2. Draw the basic outline of the table.

3. Shade the table and add a few details, like bars that stabilize the table legs.

4. Add a flower vase on top.

TWO-POINT PERSPECTIVE: HOUSE

When you want to see an angle of an object, use two-point perspective.

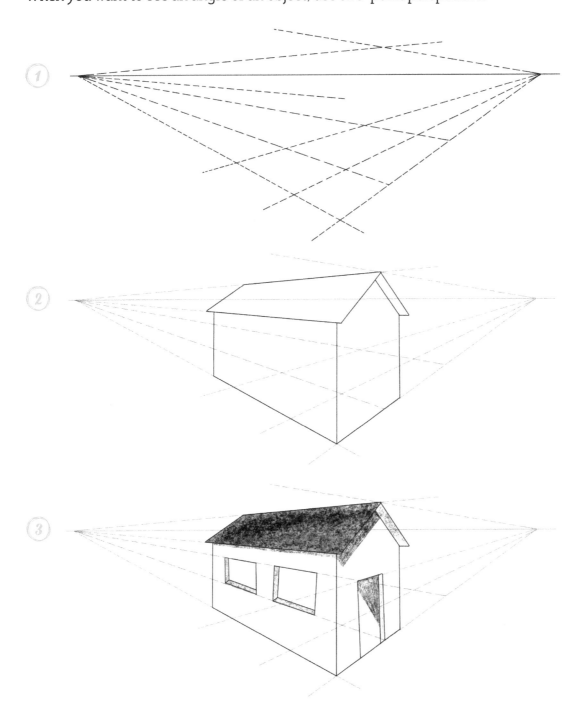

1. Create guidelines leading from two VPs on the horizon for the roof and the base corner. They don't have to be perfect—they're just helping you place the house.

2. Draw the basic shape of the house. It's easiest to start at the bottom corner and then develop the rest.

3. Add shading and details.

TWO-POINT PERSPECTIVE: OBJECTS

Try drawing a book, a treasure chest, and a shopping bag. Note that the book is above the horizon, the shopping bag is on the horizon, and the treasure chest is below the horizon.

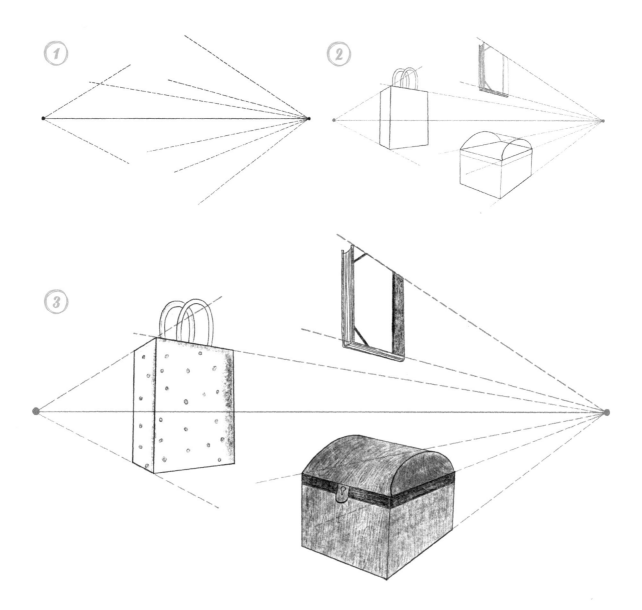

1. Start by drawing guidelines.

2. Add the basic shapes.

3. Add details and shading.

TWO-POINT PERSPECTIVE: STREET CORNER

This is one of the most familiar examples of two-point perspective: a street corner with stores.

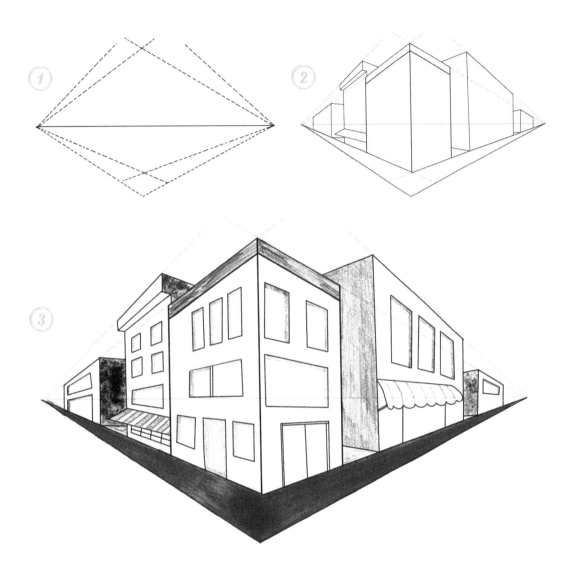

1. Draw some guidelines above and below the horizon, using two VPs.

2. Add the basic structures. To make it easier, think of them as boxes.

3. Add details like windows, trim, roofs, and awnings. Add shading.

PART TWO

Draw Everything!

SPEAK OUT

3D Letters

BASIC PRINCIPLES OF 3D LETTERING

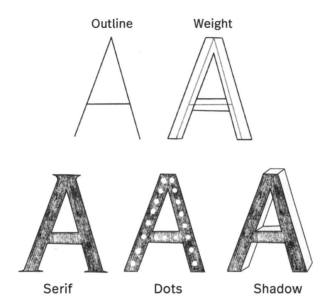

3D letters are used for making words stand out. They are great for projects, invitations, headers, banners, and more. To draw a 3D letter, all you have to do is draw your letter, add weight on the structure, and then the fun part: details! Below, you'll see steps for drawing 3D letters and more ideas for details. The details make the difference.

Some Basic Types

1. **Serif:** A serif is a small line added to the top and/or bottom of the letter.

2. **Dots and lines:** Add dots on the body (resemble lights) and lines around parts of it.

3. **Tones:** Change the color tones on the letter.

4. **Shadow:** Add a shadow for a direct 3D focus.

5. **Highlights:** Use your eraser or white pen to create white space (can combine with a shadow).

6. **Textures:** Draw different patterns and textures on the body.

SHADOW LETTERING

Adding shadows gives letters an instant 3D look. You can create shadows on any lettering style; just pick a side (left or right) and create a parallel version. Shadow letters are great for project titles.

1. Write the letters nice and big. It can be slightly messy since this outline will be erased later.

2. Add weight on each letter by using the outline as the outer edge.

3. Erase the outline and emphasize the edges.

4. Add anchor lines on the right of each letter. Straight lines have straight anchor lines; curved lines (as in the O) have slightly curved anchor lines.

5. Using the anchor lines, draw new lines parallel to the letter body.

6. Color in the shadow areas with your pencil.

7. Add parallel lines within the letter body as a finishing touch; these are called mirror lines. You can also add other details, like dots, lines, and tones.

MAKE YOUR HANDWRITING POP!

Creating letters isn't hard. You can use your regular handwriting as a base and invent your own lettering style. The best part is that you'll come up with something different every time, since handwriting changes as you grow up.

1. Write a word in pencil. It can be in cursive or print form.

2. Draw around your handwriting, to make the edges thicker. Use a pen if you like. Erase your original handwriting when done.

3. In this example, the shadows are on the left side of the word. Draw the shadow lines as shown.

4. Add small lines on the shadows. Isn't that cute?

ARTIST TIP
You can add details (dots, lines, color) on the letters themselves and draw some doodles around them to make them look even cuter.

RIBBON LETTERING

Ribbon lettering is where it looks like the letters are made from ribbons. Note that it isn't all one ribbon—it's easier to draw smaller sections. This project will help you practice detail and adding shadows to create contrast.

1. Write your word in pencil with gaps between the letters. Add looping lines wherever possible to add "movement" to the ribbon structure later. Here, you can see loops on l, b, and t.

2. Add weight around the outline. The ribbon is all the same width, but where it turns it can look thinner, so it's okay to draw some parts thinner than others.

3. Darken the outline, with pen if you like, and add small circles wherever the lines loop into another direction (e.g., look at the top and bottom of the c). Erase your original penciled word.

4. Add shading with your pencil. The front parts of the ribbon should have a thin line of shading on the right edge, and the sections of ribbon in the background should be shaded darker at each end. It gets easier with practice!

CACTUS LETTERING

Sometimes a subject can inspire the style of lettering. Cactus is a fun example.

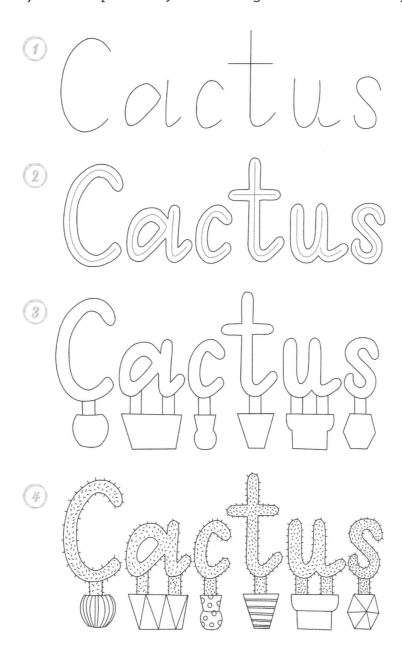

1. Sketch out the letters in pencil, leaving a slight gap in the curves of a and u. You'll see why in the next step.

2. Add weight on each letter. Make the edges rounded. Erase the initial sketch when you're satisfied.

3. Add a cactus "stem" and a pot to each letter. The pots can be different sizes and shapes. Some letters need two stems (a, u).

4. Draw prickers and decorate the pots.

TANGLED UP

Knots and Designs

BASIC PRINCIPLES OF KNOTTED DESIGNS

Knotted designs have been around for millennia and are really cool to draw. A classic knotted design usually has these characteristics:

A. It is made of one or multiple continuous loops.

B. It gives the illusion that the lines overlap.

C. It usually has a sense of symmetry.

The endless knot is a cultural symbol signifying that life is eternal, with no beginning or end.

The triquetra (or trinity knot) is a Celtic-style knot that symbolizes unity.

Endless knot

Triquetra

Celtic Knot Basics

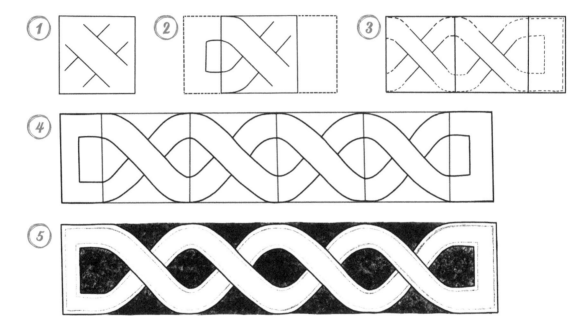

1. This is a single square unit of a knot. Imagine it as two strips overlapping to form a cross. Multiple units can be joined to create a full knot strand.

2. To create the end of the strand, we use a half-square.

3. Draw units next to each other and join them with curves. To finish the strand, use a half-square to connect the top end of the loop with the bottom.

4. This is a two-line strand with both ends joined together.

5. Add pencil shading behind it and lines in the loops to emphasize the overlapping lines.

FOUR-STRAND CELTIC KNOT

Now let's intertwine four strands. It's easier than it sounds. Once you master the four-strand Celtic knot, you can make knots with many strands and unique designs.

1. Draw six square units as shown and add half-squares at the ends.

2. Draw some rough guidelines to show how the strands weave over and under each other. Take a close look at the example if you're not sure.

3. Define your guidelines.

4. Join the strands with loops. The loops can come outside the square outline if you like. Erase the square guidelines.

5. Shade the space behind the loops to provide depth and add thin shading lines on the edges of the strands.

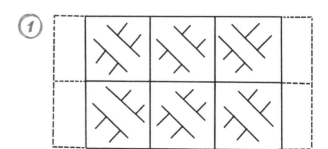

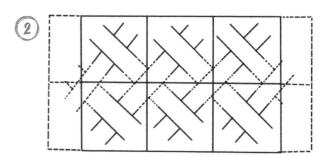

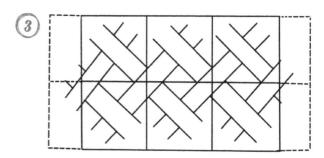

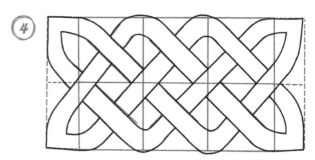

DRAW A TRIQUETRA WITH CIRCLE KNOT

This classic Celtic knot uses an intertwining triangle and circle to create an intriguing shape.

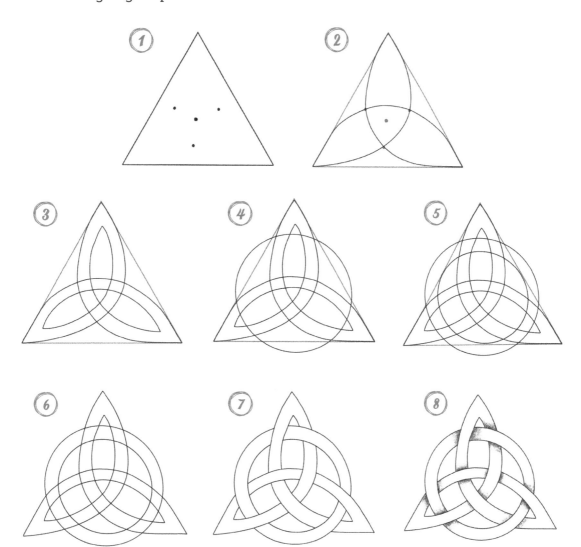

1. Draw a triangle and add a point in the center. Add three dots to mark the midpoint of each triangle line.

2. Draw a long curve between adjacent triangle points. Each curve passes through two midpoint dots.

3. Add an inner curve to each of the three long curves.

4. Draw a circle.

5. Draw an inner circle.

6. Erase the triangle guidelines.

7. Erase lines as shown to make the loops overlap.

8. Add shading where the lines go under.

CELTIC SHAPE STACKS

If the knots feel too complicated, try this exercise. Celtic stacks are traditionally created by interlocking shapes. Let's put a twist on this by using different shapes and adding patterns.

①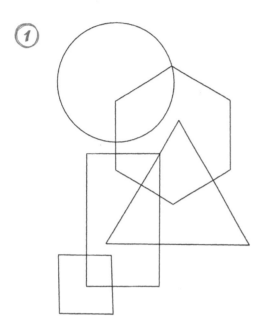

②

③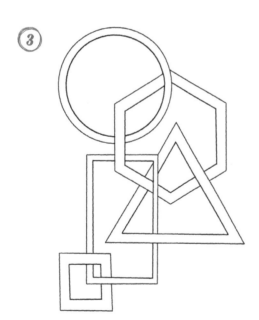

④

1. Draw different shapes that intersect.

2. Add an outline to each one.

3. Erase lines so they form overlapping lines.

4. Add patterns.

HEART PENDANTS WITH TWO, THREE, AND FOUR LOOPS

Here are three ways of creating a heart-shaped pendant using two (infinity heart), three (trinity heart), or four (classic love heart) loops.

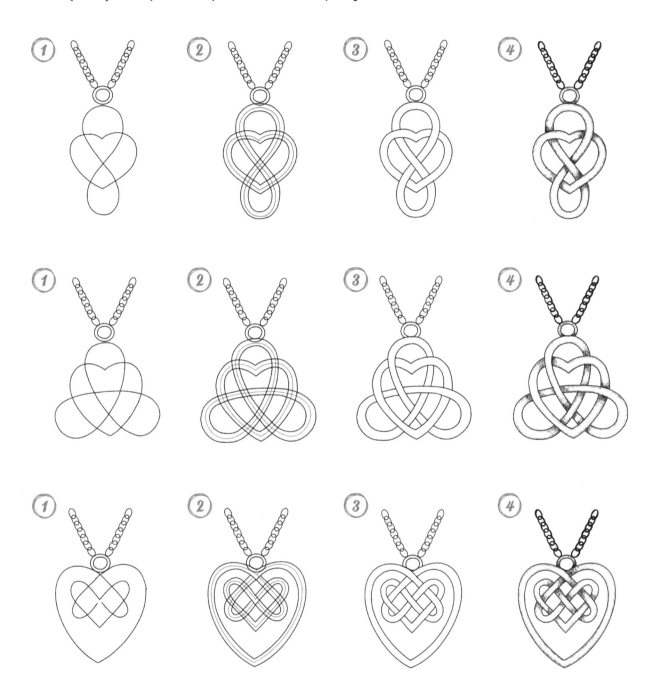

1. Draw a heart and add two, three, or four loops.

2. Add weight around the outline.

3. Erase parts to make the lines overlap.

4. Add shading and define the necklace chain.

Optical Illusions

BASIC PRINCIPLES OF OPTICAL ILLUSIONS

An optical illusion tricks you into seeing something different from what's actually there. Some optical illusions use color, shape, line, patterns, light, and shadow to achieve the illusion. Drawing techniques for creating them involve a lot of overlapping lines, erasing lines, and defining them with shadow and light.

Here are some examples:

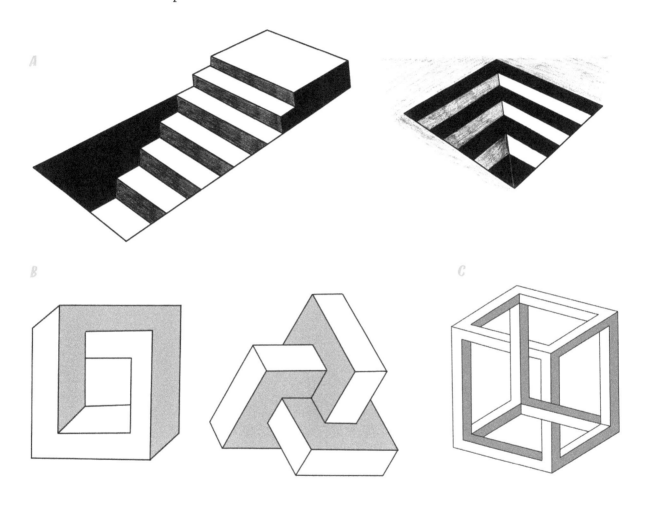

A. Anamorphic illusions like this 3D staircase and hole appear to be rising into and out of the paper.

B. Impossible shapes appear to be 3D, but if you look closer, you can see that they are in fact 2D and impossible to exist in real life.

C. The Escher Cube (or Impossible Cube) is a popular optical illusion.

ENDLESS STAIRCASE

The endless staircase appears to be a continuous loop of stairs. If you were on it, you would just keep climbing and never get any higher.

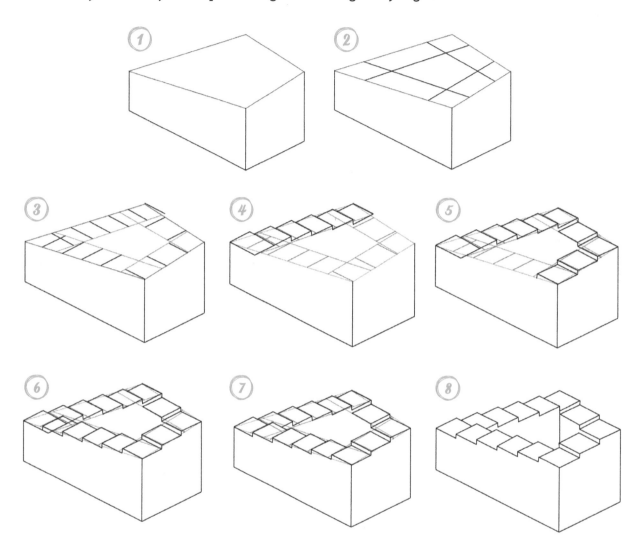

1. Draw a rough kite-shaped box.

2. Add crossing lines on the top.

3. Now make steps. Note that the shorter edges of the box have three steps; the longer edges have six steps where the last lines overlap.

4. Start drawing the steps as seen in the image.

5. Draw the steps on the shorter edges as shown.

6. Next, draw the steps for the second long side. Make the final step overlap the first one.

7. Erase the overlapping lines.

8. Erase the guidelines and draw a vertical line as shown to complete the endless staircase.

IMPOSSIBLE TRIANGLE

An impossible triangle is a great example of making a 2D drawing look 3D. Even though you know it's just a flat drawing, its twists and turns and shadows create a great illusion.

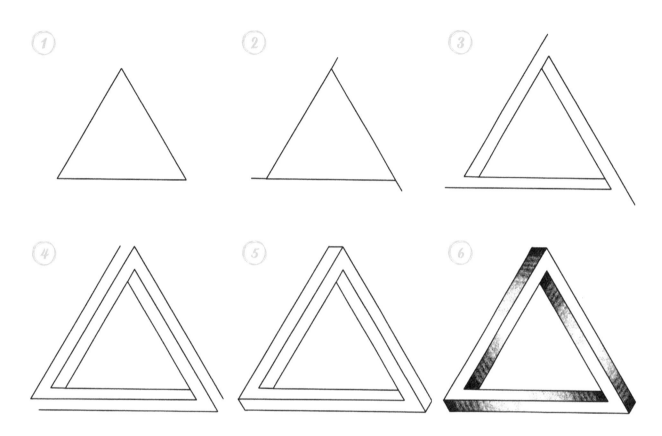

1. Draw a triangle with three equal sides.

2. Extend each side with a short line.

3. Draw lines parallel to the triangle, starting from the outer point of the short lines.

4. Add a second set of parallel lines.

5. Add short lines to join the parallel sides.

6. Shade the drawing.

DRAW A THREE-PRONG ILLUSION

This is another optical illusion you can easily learn. It's fun because you start off with a few simple lines and then suddenly you're drawing something 3D.

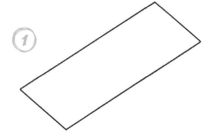

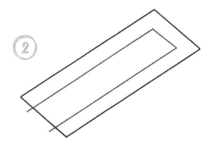

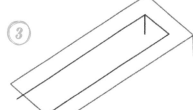

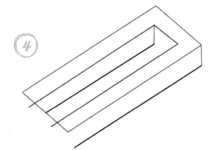

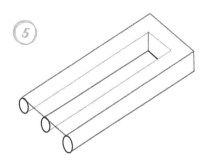

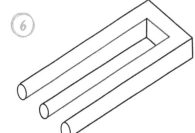

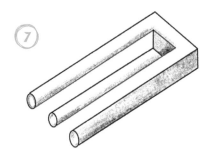

1. Start with a tilted rectangle.

2. Draw two parallel lines starting inside the rectangle but extending outside. Join the inner ends with a short line.

3. Add two vertical lines.

4. From the end point of each vertical line, draw two parallel lines.

5. Add three ovals.

6. Erase the guidelines and darken the image.

7. Add shading to provide depth.

CREATING 3D OBJECTS WITH LINES

This fun exercise uses lines and curves to give an illusion that an object is behind the lines.

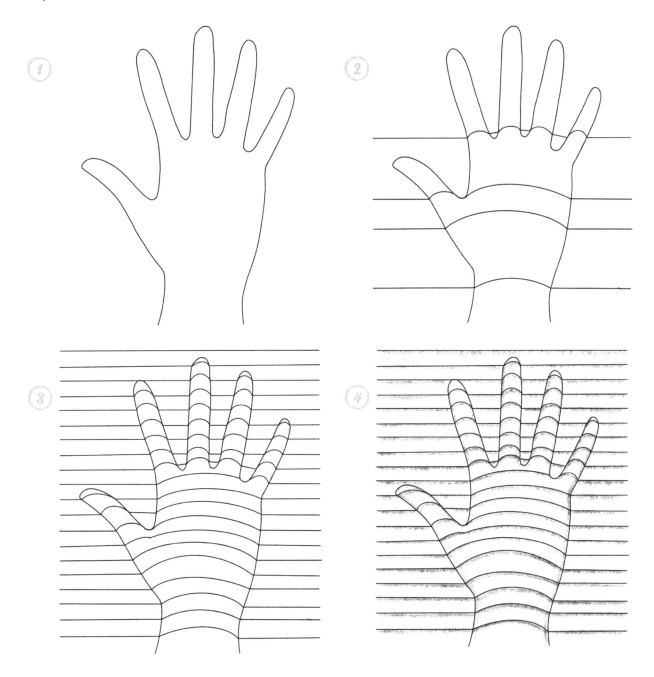

1. Draw an outline of a hand (or any other object).

2. Draw lines that curve when inside the hand but are straight when outside.

3. Continue this pattern from top to bottom.

4. Shade around the hand and under each line.

DRAW FOR LAUGHS

Cartoons

BASIC PRINCIPLES FOR DRAWING CARTOONS

Cartoons are more than just funny. They are a powerful way to get through to anyone. You may have seen cartoons in newspapers or graphic novels; or gag cartoons, animated cartoons, and even caricatures. You can create cartoons of people, animals, objects, nature—anything! The secret is expression.

See how you can use different expressions to make a drawing come alive and tell a story:

Naughty boy:
"How can I make school more inter-esting today?"

Shocked boy:
"The video game stopped working! Now what?"

Thoughtful boy:
"So, do aliens actually exist?"

Smiling boy:
"I love taking my puppy for walks!"

Now, let's take it one step further. Let's use the same expressions but change the hairstyles to turn this character into different female characters. Note that female characters usually have prominent eyelashes, thinner and pointier eyebrows, and pronounced lips.

Bully girl:
"Give me your lunch money . . . or else."

Shocked actress:
"Oh no, the monster's coming this way!"

Doubtful girl:
"Teacher, my cat really did eat my homework!"

Smiling mom:
"I'm so glad my son ate his greens today."

DRAW KIDS

A bit of roundness (chubby cheeks and limbs, for instance) gives cartoon kids a youthful softness. They have wide eyes and happy smiles, too.

Follow these examples for each cartoon kid:

1. Sketch the shapes as shown.

2. Erase the outline enough so you can still just see it. Draw the details. Note how the eyes have two small circles as highlights. Erase the rest of the outline.

3. Darken the final image and add shading.

DRAW ANIME

Anime is a very popular cartoon style. Some of the characteristic features are pointed face, tiny nose, triangular mouth, and emphatic hairstyle.

1. Draw a basic face shape, neck, and shoulders. The head is quite big, but the chin is small and sharp.

2. Mark a large portion of the head as the hair, with a floppy fringe. Add an outline of the other features. Eyes are larger than life.

3. The eyebrows show even through the hair. Define the features. Add big irises with lots of little light dots to the eyes.

4. Add some shading and define the eyes well.

ANIMAL AND OBJECT CARTOONS

You can make an object come to life simply by giving it a face, or you can give an animal a personality by having it perform a human activity. Here are examples of a car grinning and a bird painting.

1. Add basic shape.   2. Draw more details.   3. Erase guidelines and shade.

More Examples for You to Try:

Make inanimate objects
lively and fun.

Here are some more animals
with their own characteristics.

INVENT YOUR OWN CHARACTER

Come up with some keywords to invent your own character. For example, a bookworm farm girl. You can try this exercise (and even have a story in your mind) to create many unique characters.

1. Sketch basic shapes for the head, torso, and arms.

2. Draw a table line and a book. Add details on the girl: braids, shirt, hand(s).

3. Erase the guidelines and define the girl's features and the book.

4. Darken the final sketch lines.

HOME SWEET HOME
Buildings

BASIC PRINCIPLES FOR DRAWING BUILDINGS

There are many ways to draw a building. You can also combine different styles and even come up with your own.

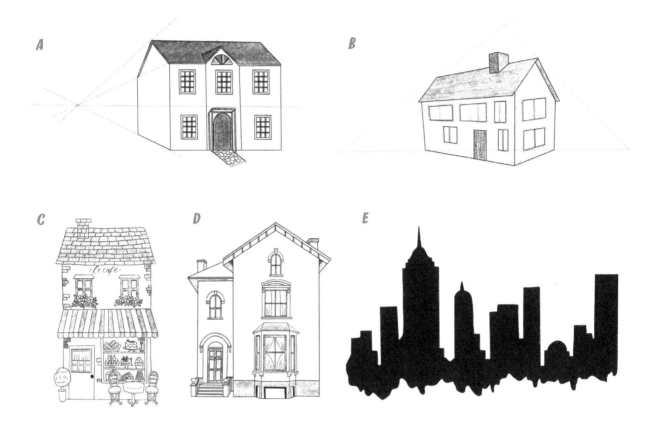

A. **One-point perspective:** A vanishing point on the horizon is used to create diverging guidelines. The guidelines are used to create a structure. A good way to remember: One-point perspective shows one main angle of an object.

B. **Two-point perspective:** Two-point perspective shows two sides of the house at a prominent angle, using two vanishing points on the horizon.

C. **Flat cartoon style:** This is more of a doodling approach to drawing buildings. Wavy and uneven lines create a whimsical feel.

D. **Front view:** Imagine yourself standing directly in front of a house.

E. **Silhouette:** Silhouettes are a great way to symbolize a house or collection of buildings. They're especially effective for landscapes and city skylines.

HOUSE PORTRAIT

A house portrait can be just as meaningful as a human portrait and makes a great present for family members. Take a photo of your home at a flattering angle and then draw it.

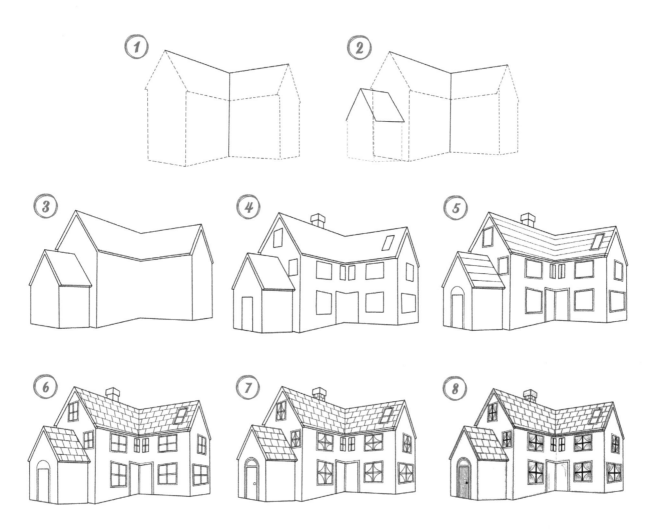

1. Start with the basic structure.

2. Add components.

3. Define the roof and house.

4. Draw the chimney and windows.

5. Add thinner lines on the edges of the roof, windows, and door frame.

6. Add alternating lines on the roof.

7. Draw curtains.

8. Shade lightly.

CASTLE

Drawing a castle is easy if you imagine it as a bunch of cylinders with cones on top, all stacked together. You can customize it with some simple touches.

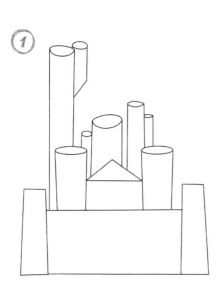

1. Draw a rectangle, then add shapes: cylinders, triangles, rectangles, etc.

2. Add cones on top of the cylinders and windows in different sizes.

3. Draw more details.

4. Define the shapes and shade lightly.

ARTIST TIP
The turrets (castle towers) can be made more interesting: Add flags, metal pikes, staircases, an attached small tower, balcony, and as many windows as you like.

BUILDING BANNER DESIGN

Try wrapping a banner around some buildings. You can add banners around any object, but this city full of buildings looks really snug all wrapped up.

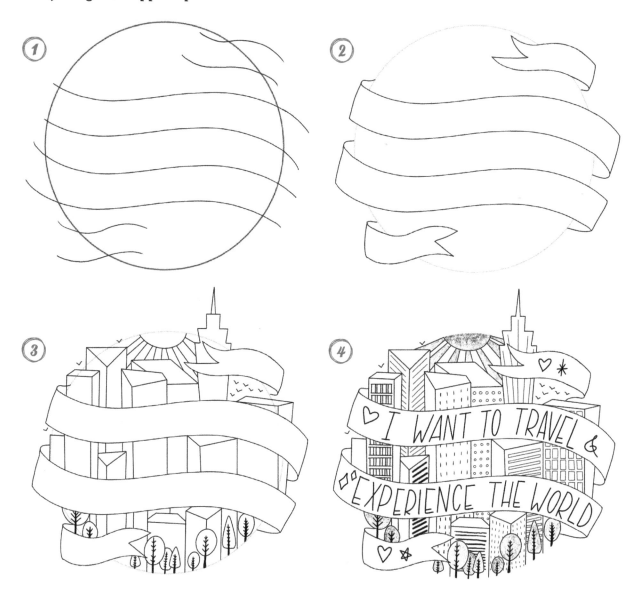

1. Start with a circle. Draw some wavy pairs of lines.

2. Join the ends and create loops to form the banner.

3. Add buildings in different shapes and sizes, along with some trees, the sun, and birds to give it a vibrant cartoony feel.

4. Shade and define the details (windows in interesting shapes) and add a quote on the banner. You could add little doodles, like stars and hearts, to make it even cuter.

LIGHTHOUSES (OLD AND NEW)

A lighthouse is basically a large cylinder with a little house attached. Let's make two: a new, sleek lighthouse and an old, crumbling one. You can use this technique to convert any building from new to old, like making a haunted house or an abandoned farmhouse.

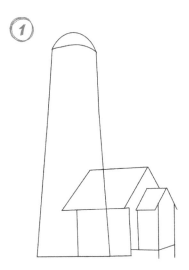

1. Start with the basic shapes.

2. Define the shapes a bit more.

3. Add shading around the edges.

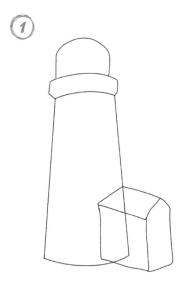

1. Start with the basic shapes. They can be a little rounded and rough.

2. Add definition. Make your lines a little wavy to suggest that the building is crumbling.

3. Time to add the "old" details: exposed brick and cracks in the walls.

GO GREEN

Plants, Trees, and Nature

BASIC PRINCIPLES FOR DRAWING NATURE

Plants give us life and also provide us a standard for beauty. Nature is a common topic for artists—especially leaves and trees. They are also great for practicing drawing because you can find them anywhere to use as a reference.

Here's a basic formula for drawing leaves:

1. Draw a curved line.

2. Double it.

3. Add curved lines to make the leaf shape.

4. Draw leaf veins.

5. Add some shading on the edges.

Add Details to Make Many Types of Leaves:

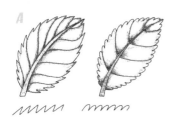

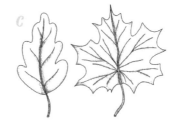

A. Draw patterned outlines. You can make them neat or slightly irregular.

B. Create multiple clusters of leaves.

C. Vary the shape. Leaves can be rounded or pointed. Veins help define the shape.

D. Make the leaf fat or thin.

DRAW TREES

Trees come in many different shapes and sizes, but the structure is always the same; they have a wood base and a leafy cover.

You already learned how to draw a coconut tree in activity 3. But it's good to be able to draw different types.

1. Draw two concave lines.

2. Draw a "V" over them.

3. Draw branches.

4. Draw basic shapes to create the leaf base.

5. Draw a rough curving outline around the shapes.

ARTIST TIP

A way to remember how to draw branches: They resemble the letters Y, F, and V.

Add Details to Create Different Trees:

A. Draw a tree with more branches, or fewer.

B. Change the height. Some trees are tall, and some are short.

C. Vary the shapes of the leaf areas and the trunk.

D. Create different leafy body shapes. You can stack them to add volume.

DRAW A PINE TREE

You can use pine trees in many ways: as elements in landscapes, in holiday cards (just add decorations and a star), or simply for daily drawing practice.

1. Start with a triangle and two lines under it.

2. Divide the triangle into parts, with the top having many smaller sections.

3. Draw a free outline using the sections as a guide.

4. Add lines extending inward from each of the tree points, to create volume.

5. Under the extending lines, darken areas with pencil.

6. Add lighter shading on the edges and on the tree trunk. For a summer look, shade it darker. Leaving portions white creates a snowy pine tree.

FLOWERS AND HOUSEPLANTS

Flowers and houseplants offer a lot of variety when it comes to drawing. Try this simple way to draw a rose and cactus:

1. Start by drawing the basic shapes.

2. Add details to form petals and folds.

3. Erase guidelines and shade lightly.

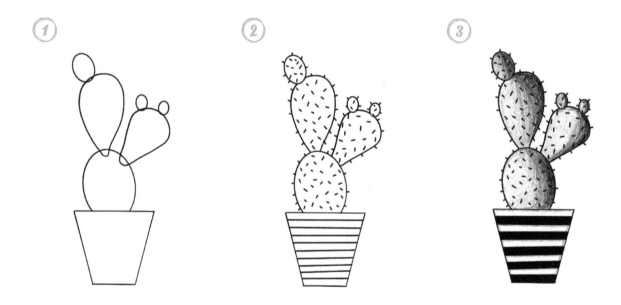

1. Draw the basic outline (rough ovals in different sizes).

2. Add details (prickers and details on the pot).

3. Add volume by shading.

More Examples for You to Try:

A. Houseplants are fun to draw. You can also use references from your house and photos to practice.

B. Flowers are beautiful, offering variety and color. You can combine them with other elements, too, as shown.

C. Combine terrariums, collections of plants, and animals to add more interest.

Flowers can be drawn in many ways. You can play around with angles and create many variations.

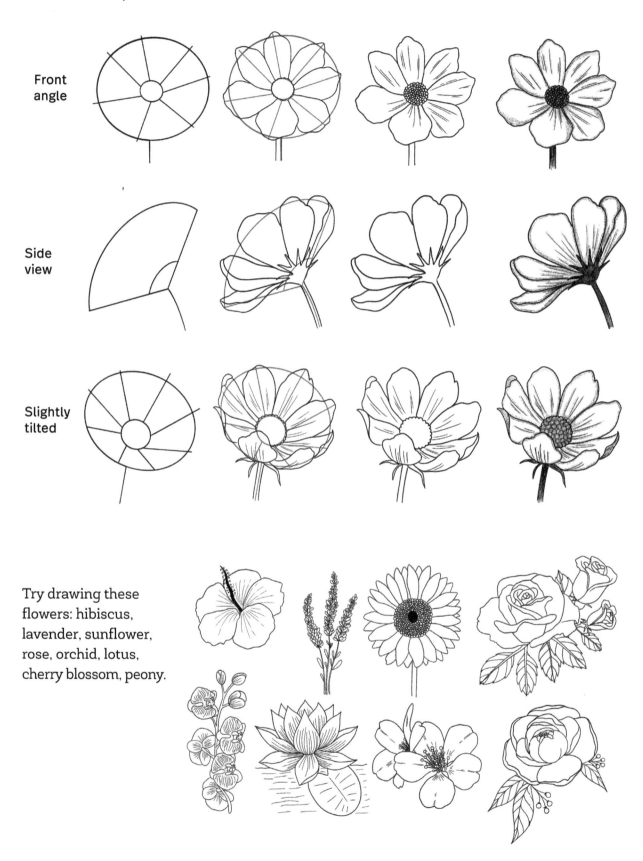

Front angle

Side view

Slightly tilted

Try drawing these flowers: hibiscus, lavender, sunflower, rose, orchid, lotus, cherry blossom, peony.

DRAW A LEAFY WREATH

Wreaths are perfect for doodling on cards, invitations, project covers, and party favors. Here's an easy one to try:

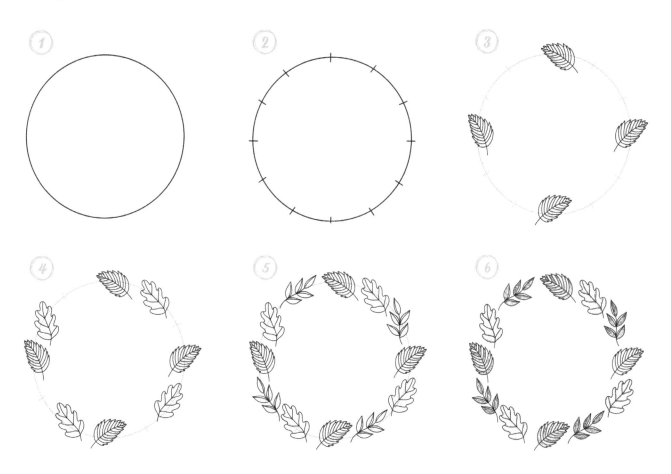

1. Draw a circle.

2. Imagine this is a clock and mark twelve points. Start with 12, 3, 6, and 9, and fill in the rest.

3. Draw one leaf design on points 12, 3, 6, and 9.

4. Draw a different style leaf on points 1, 4, 7, and 10.

5. Draw a third leaf design on points 2, 5, 8, and 11.

6. Erase the circle guideline and shade lightly.

EVERYTHING THE EYE CAN SEE
Landscapes

BASIC PRINCIPLES FOR DRAWING LANDSCAPES

There's a method to drawing landscapes that's easy to learn, and then you can break the rules to come up with your own versions. Landscapes are usually imagined within a shape, like a rectangle or square. Here are the components:

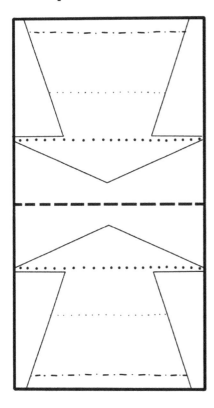

As you can see, the rectangle is divided into sections. The finished rectangle is an example of a landscape. In each section, you can add details:

A. Trees

B. Clouds

C. Mountains and other natural structures (canyons, plateaus, etc.)

D. Animals

E. Bodies of water

F. Buildings (cabins, cottages, etc.)

G. Rocks

H. Sun, moon, and stars

TRIPTYCH

A triptych is a piece of art divided into three parts. Often, the three parts depict different objects or are drawn from a different perspective, but here we focus on the reflection of the landscape in the lake.

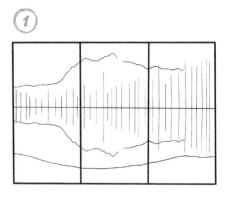

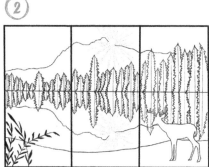

1. Use a full sheet of paper (A3 is great). Divide the paper into three sections. Draw a horizon line and add a mountain and straight lines for the trees. To make the reflection, copy them below the horizon. Add another line near the bottom of the page to denote the lake edge.

2. Add a sun with its rays spreading from the side of the mountain. Draw outlines of pine trees. Invert them below the horizon to create the reflection.

3. Add shading on the trees and sun, and shade the reflection more lightly. This creates the illusion of the reflection. Add some weeds and an animal at the bottom corners of the page to suggest land. After this, you can cut the sections and display them on the wall with a gap between each.

LANDSCAPES IN SHAPES

You can come up with many landscape concepts centered around a particular shape. If the shape is divided, draw different scenes in each part. Here are a few ideas.

For each shape:

1. Draw an outline.

2. Draw a scene within the outline.

3. Add details and shade with pencil.

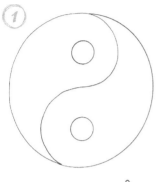

A DIFFERENT PERSPECTIVE

You can add a new spin on a landscape by using a secret weapon: perspective! Adding an open window gives you the illusion of standing in a room looking out.

1. Draw a rectangle and add a window frame and a window opened out.

2. Add details such as plants near the window, and trees, sand, sea, rocks, and mountains in the distance. Notice how objects close to the window are proportionately larger than objects far away.

3. Shade lightly and pencil in more details such as wood textures on the window frame and veins on the leaves.

ISLAND IN A TEACUP

Landscapes can be extremely versatile. We usually think of them in a realistic style, but you can draw them in surreal, cute, and conceptual ways. Imagine an island in a transparent teacup!

1. Start by drawing a teacup and saucer.

2. Add a mountain structure at the top that extends up from a rocky base. Draw clouds.

3. Add details: hot-air balloon, windmill, houses, sheep, trees, and bushes. Draw

a whale underwater breathing out bubbles and add a tea bag on the side of the cup. Erase any lines from the teacup and saucer that overlap the new details.

4. Finish by adding some birds, decorating the tea bag, and lightly shading.

16

WALK ON THE WILD SIDE
Animals

BASIC PRINCIPLES FOR DRAWING ANIMALS

Animals are great fun to draw because you can depict them in many ways. Here are a few styles to get you started.

A. **Realistic style:** When you draw animals in a realistic style you keep the proportions of the animal. Shading and highlights make the animal stand out on the page.

B. **Quirky cartoon style:** Animals can be drawn in funny ways, too. You can imagine them doing human things, like these bees sharing a cup of tea or this bear dressed as a clown riding a bicycle with his bunny friend.

C. **Flat scrapbook style:** Use a scrapbook-inspired style to draw an animal and add cute designs around it. Draw the outline and color in with solid tones. This toucan has a 2D feel to it.

HORSES

Horses are considered to be one of the most difficult animals to draw, which is why they're included here. But they're not that hard. Try this tutorial and see for yourself.

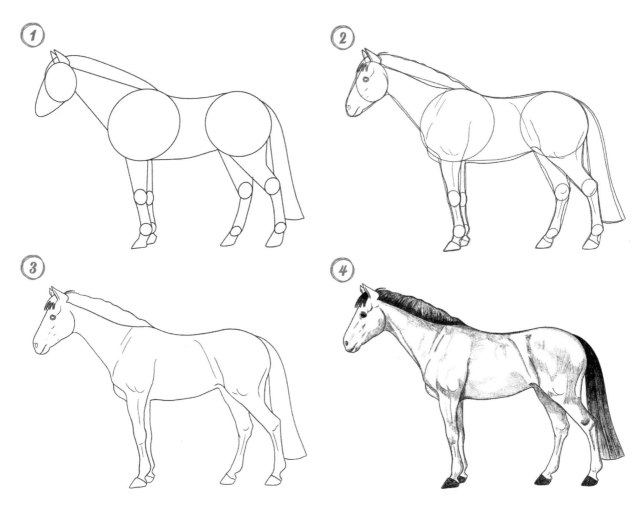

1. Draw the basic shapes for the body.

2. Draw around the guidelines: head, legs, mane, and tail.

3. Erase the guidelines.

4. Shade with pencil.

ARTIST TIP You can draw a zebra by drawing a horse and adding stripes.

ARTIST TIP Try drawing a horse at different angles. This one is drawn from a front-facing perspective. It looks like the horse is cantering toward you.

WILDCATS: JAGUARS AND MORE

Here's a tutorial on how to draw a jaguar. You can apply this technique when drawing other big cats.

1. Draw a basic outline. Use a triangle for the face and circles for the body and paws.

2. Define the body around the guidelines.

3. Erase the guidelines and add spots all over. Add detail to the face.

4. Color in the spots and shade lightly.

ARTIST TIP

When drawing the spot clusters, imagine each cluster like a broken circle with a few scattered dots on it. Jaguars and leopards have similar spots.

Use this basic body shape and change the face and details to draw other beautiful wildcats.

A. A tiger has thin, wavy stripes.

B. A panther has a longer face and can have spots or be plain.

C. A lynx has fewer spots and marks on the body and distinctive pointy ears.

D. A cheetah has small, irregular spots.

CARTOON ANIMALS ACTING HUMAN

Try drawing animals doing human things. You can come up with more ideas than what's included here. Just think of an animal and draw it doing an activity you like to do, like playing a game or watching TV.

For all three drawings:

1. Start with the basic outline.

2. Define the shapes.

3. Erase the guidelines and add shading.

CUTE AND QUIRKY ANIMALS

Try drawing animals in a fun cartoon style and play around with pencil textures. This creates a scrapbook, 2D feel, and is great for cards and doodling when you don't want to worry about the proportions and just have fun! Here are a tiger and a chicken:

More Examples for You to Try:

UNICORNS AND MORE
Magical Creatures

BASIC PRINCIPLES FOR DRAWING MAGICAL CREATURES

Magical creatures are whatever you want them to be. They can resemble animals, humans, or even be enchanted objects. It is helpful to use a real subject as the basis of the drawing, then add the "magic" component.

A. **Magical animals:** Pictured here is a griffin, a mix of an eagle and a lion. You can combine physical traits of animals to create your own hybrid. Folktales are filled with such creatures.

B. **Magical humanoid creatures:** Fairies, elves, nymphs, leprechauns, pixies, and half-human monsters all have human traits as a base. Here is a fairy who is relatively bigger than the butterfly.

C. **Magical or enchanted objects:** An egg becomes a dragon's egg. A magic mirror can see, move, and talk. You can change the properties of regular objects to support your illustration, or make an object come alive.

DRAW A DRAGON

There are both good and bad dragons in stories, but which-ever they are, they are always impressive. And not that difficult to draw!

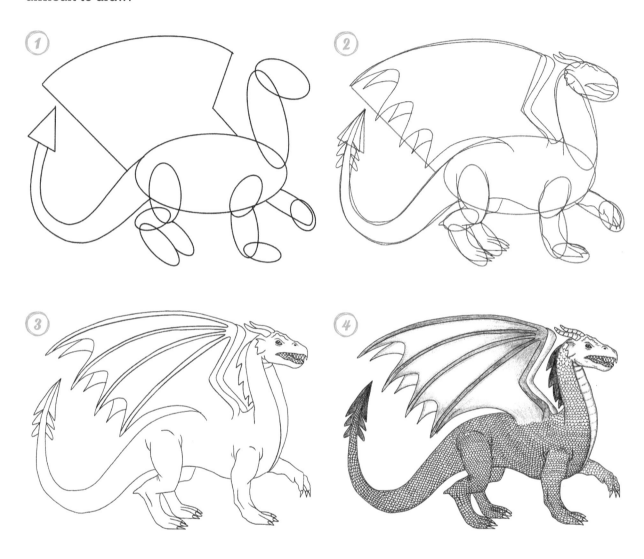

1. Draw the basic shapes.

2. Define the details: head, legs, wings, and tail.

3. Erase the guidelines and add teeth, nose, and eyes to the dragon's face. Add creases at the tops of the limbs, too. What about your dragon's skin? Take a look at the artist tip.

4. Finish by adding some shading.

ARTIST TIP These textures can be used to accentuate dragon skin: scales, small lines, zigzags, rows of lines.

DRAW A VAMPIRE AND WITCH

Here's a step-by-step guide for these spooky characters.

1. Draw a basic body shape.

2. Add details: pointy teeth, wide eyes, exaggerated hairstyle, cape, and bow tie.

3. Add definition by shading.

1. Draw the basic outline of the body, bird, and cauldron.

2. Add details: hat, outfit, face, feathers on the bird, bubbles in the cauldron.

3. Add definition by shading.

DRAW A UNICORN IN DIFFERENT STYLES

There are many ways you can draw one thing. Try the style challenge with a unicorn.
For the full unicorn or just the head and neck:

1. Draw the basic shapes.

3. Erase the guidelines.

2. Add details.

4. Shade with pencil.

Some Other Ways to Depict a Unicorn:

| Unicorn with wreath | Cute cartoon unicorn | Unicorn with banner | Unicorn with leafy doodles |

DRAW A MERMAID

You can draw mermaids facing you or turned away to highlight their flowing hair and their most distinctive feature: their tail.

1. Plot out the body with shapes. Notice that it's a free-flowing form.

2. Add details such as the hair (mermaids usually have long, flowing tresses) and design the tail the way you want it.

3. Shade and define.

1. Sketch the basic structure, focusing on the back and tail.

2. Add a large section of hair and define the shapes.

3. Shade lightly and draw scales and lines on the tail.

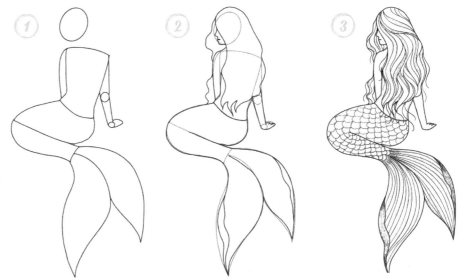

Hands

BASIC PRINCIPLES FOR DRAWING HANDS

Hands may seem daunting to draw, but they are easy enough if you just get started. Here are some tips:

1. **Use photo references:** Copy them until you feel comfortable.

2. **Observe your own hands:** Look at the curves, angles, and movement.

3. **Practice drawing hands:** Do this as often as you can.

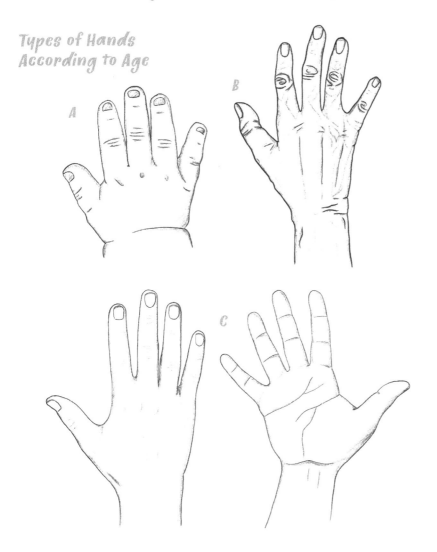

Types of Hands According to Age

ARTIST TIP

If you're unsure about drawing hands, don't worry. The oldest trick in the book is to hide the hands in pockets or cross the arms. The man here has one hand in his pocket and the other hand is placed in a side view (easier to draw!). The woman has her arms crossed with a partial view of fingers.

A. Baby hands are adorably small, rounded, and stubby.

B. Old hands have prominent veins and more lines all over, and fingers are sometimes crooked.

C. Developed adult hands have a smooth texture with faint lines for the knuckles, palm, and finger joints.

DRAW HANDS

There are many ways to draw hands, and you'll discover what works best for you. Try different techniques until you find your sweet spot.

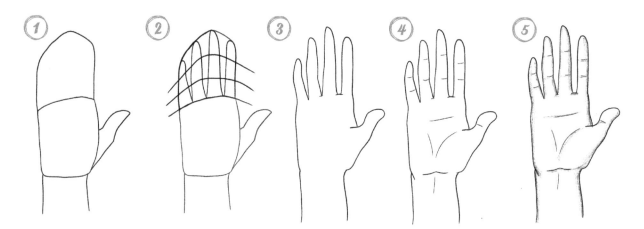

1. Start with a mitten shape.

2. Add some lines to guide you in drawing the fingers.

3. Erase the guidelines.

4. Add lines for the joints and palm.

5. Shade around the edges. This is the glove method.

Practice Other Ways to Draw Hands:

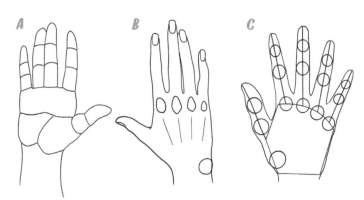

A. Sections method: Imagine the hand in sections (draw the palm first, then add the fingers).

B. Free method: Draw the fingers by estimating them, without a guideline, just using the knuckles if needed.

C. Circle joint method: Draw a rough pentagon and draw lines for the fingers. Then add circles for the joints.

ARTIST TIP When drawing hands holding objects, there are many ways to capture the result. In the first sketch, the thumb is prominent, while in the second image, the four fingers are seen but the thumb is hidden. Try holding an object and moving it around to understand the different perspectives.

SINGLE HAND GESTURES

Here are three hand gestures to try: a side view, a palm view, and a back-of-hand view.

For all three drawings:

1. Start with a basic outline.

2. Add details.

3. Erase the outline and define the drawing.

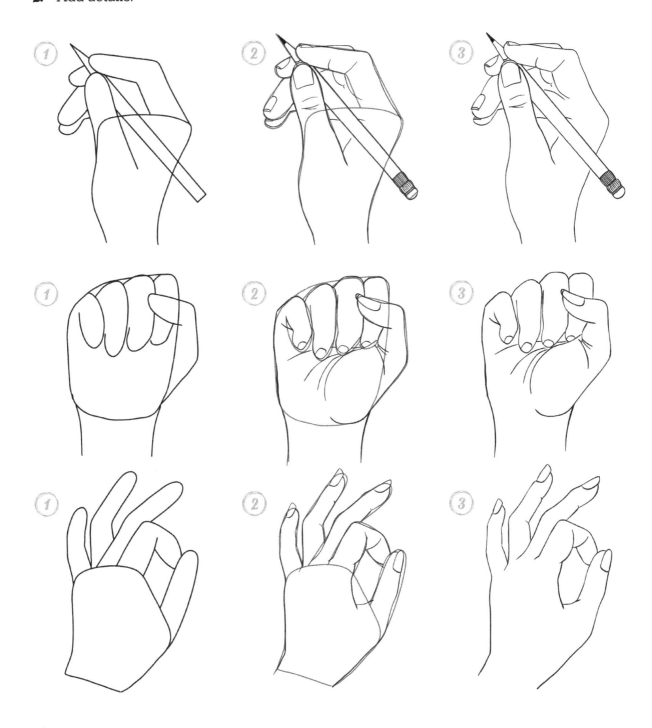

DOUBLE HAND GESTURES

Double hand gestures require a bit of attention to detail; both hands should be similar in size (unless the hands belong to two different people).

For all three drawings:

1. Start with a basic outline.

2. Add details. Erase the outline and define the drawing.

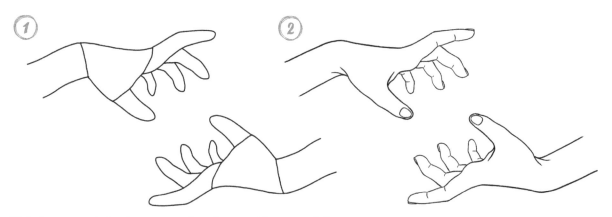

This is a magician's pose. It involves widespread fingers in a sideways view.

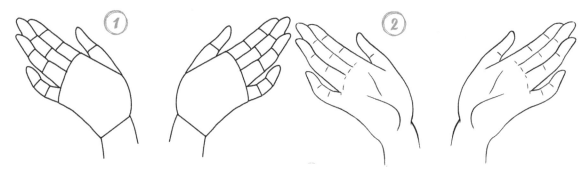

This is a clapping or a hands-open-wide pose. Notice how the fingers are slightly bent to give it a more natural gesture.

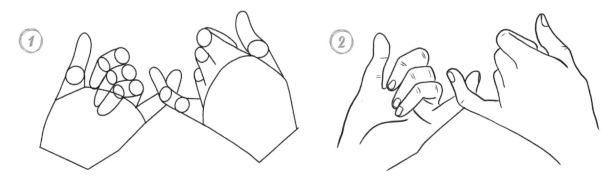

This is a "pinky swear" hand gesture. One hand is facing palm up and the other reveals the back of the hand.

HEART HANDS

Heart hands is a popular gesture that's also quite pleasing to draw. Try adding a little scenery inside the heart for an added effect.

1. Use the circle joint method to draw the basic outline of the hands.

2. Add weight to the outline.

3. Erase the guidelines.

4. Shade lightly. You can draw a little scene inside the heart; this one looks like a photo from a beach trip.

FRIENDS AND NEIGHBORS

Faces

BASIC PRINCIPLES FOR DRAWING FACES

Drawing faces is a very satisfying task. It may seem intimidating at first, so it's helpful to get used to drawing the features separately. Once you feel like you can draw them with ease, putting them all together is a piece of cake.

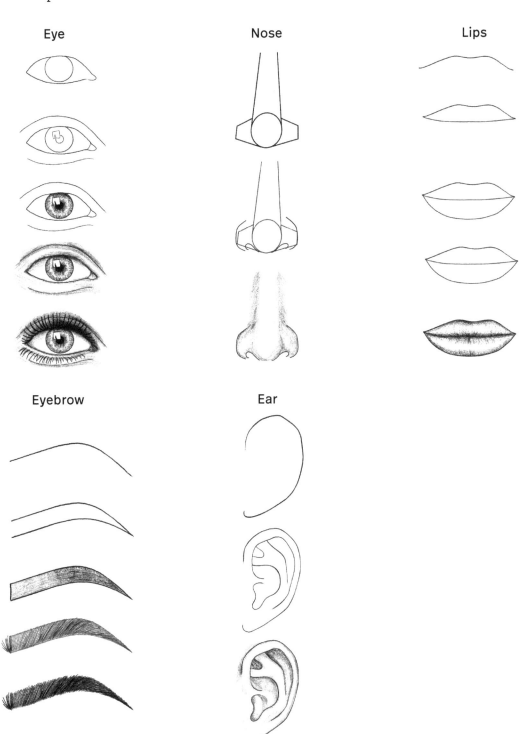

Eye

Nose

Lips

Eyebrow

Ear

BASIC FORMULA FOR DRAWING FACES

1. Draw a circle and add a cross extending below; these are the basic guidelines.

2. Add features and define the face, slowly adjusting and erasing the guidelines as you do so until you get the desired result.

Practice this regularly and you will start to see improvement.

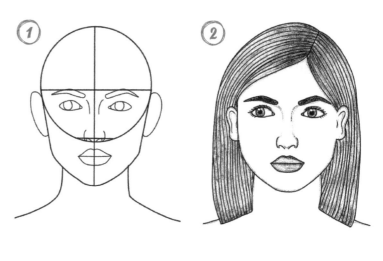

It's important to note general differences between a woman's face and a man's face. Look at this example:

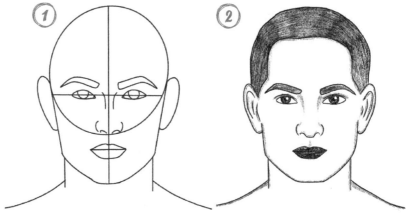

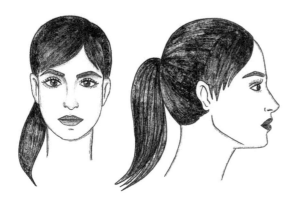

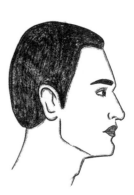

A woman's face often has a U-shape, whereas a man's facial structure often resembles an angular V. Women's faces usually have softer, rounded edges, while men's faces usually have a more robust structure. Men have an Adam's apple, while women don't.

STYLE CHALLENGE

Remember you have the freedom to draw faces exactly the way you want. This exercise shows you how to draw a face in multiple styles. Start with basic keywords to define your character: wavy, long hair; winged eyeliner; angular face. Here's one to try:

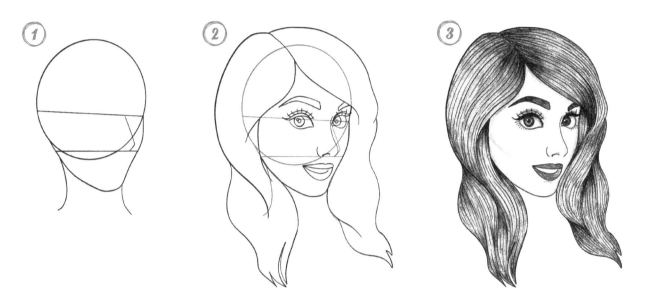

Next, let's draw this same girl in nine more different styles:

MEN

Try these examples to practice drawing male faces. You can change up skin tones and hairstyles, add a mustache or beard, etc. Men as a general rule have thicker eyebrows and more prominent jawlines than women do.

For each drawing:

1. Draw the basic outline.   **2.** Add features.   **3.** Shade and define details.

Face 1

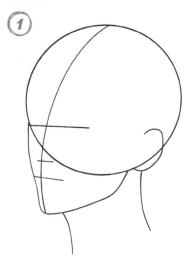 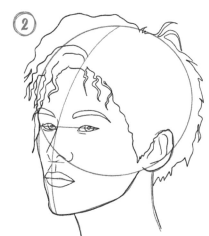 

Face 2

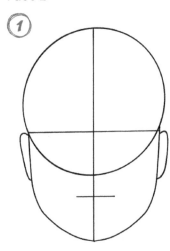  

You can create your own original characters (called OCs) by getting in the mood of drawing different faces.

Some general steps to go by: Note the distinguishing features. For example, face 1 has slightly curly, messy hair; monolid eyes (the eyelids are not creased); an angular chin; and a sharp nose. Face 2 has glasses; small eyes; thick eyebrows; a mustache and beard; a button nose; thin lips; and wavy hair.

1. Draw the basic outline.   **2.** Add features.   **3.** Shade and define details.

Face 3

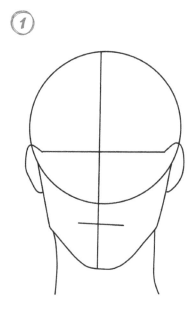  

Face 4

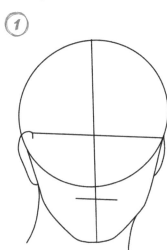 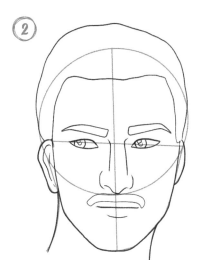 

Face 3 has a chiseled, long face; narrowed eyes; big ears; and a sideswept hairstyle. Face 4 has curly hair; a small mustache; a long nose; and wide eyes.

You can practice one face regularly until you feel confident enough to redraw it in a similar fashion. This helps you if you wish to develop a comic character and create your own comic series.

While drawing, you can also brainstorm personalities of the subject. Maybe your character likes pizza, plays the guitar, hates homework, enjoys road trips, etc. These qualities will allow a character to come to life.

WOMEN

Try these examples to practice drawing female faces. Add variety by changing up hair, skin tones, and angles of the face, and playing with features.
For each drawing:

1. Draw the basic outline. **2.** Add features. **3.** Shade and define details.

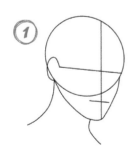  

HAIRSTYLES

Hairstyles play a key role in a person's appearance. Here are the types of hair you can draw, ranging from straight, wavy, and curly, to tightly coiled.

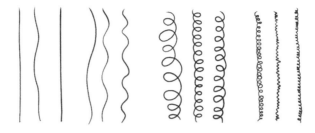

Basic formula for straight hair

Basic formula for curly hair

ARTIST TIP Divide the hair in sections and then shade on both sides. Add volume in the middle and highlights on the sides. Add loose strands for a more natural look.

More Examples for You to Try:

ALL SHAPES AND SIZES

Bodies

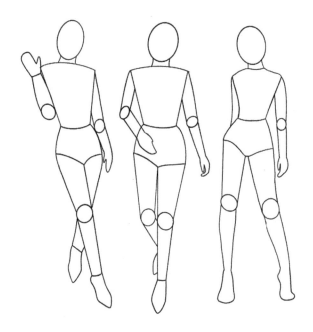

BASIC PRINCIPLES FOR DRAWING BODIES

Drawing a body is easier when you imagine it in sections. Practice will help you get the proportions right. Try copying images and then comparing those with bodies drawn from your imagination. You'll be able to see your progress with steady practice over time. Here are some examples of bodies in different poses:

SPORTS ON ICE

Try drawing the figure skater and the hockey player in these basic poses. Later, you can come up with different poses such as arms raised or legs in motion.

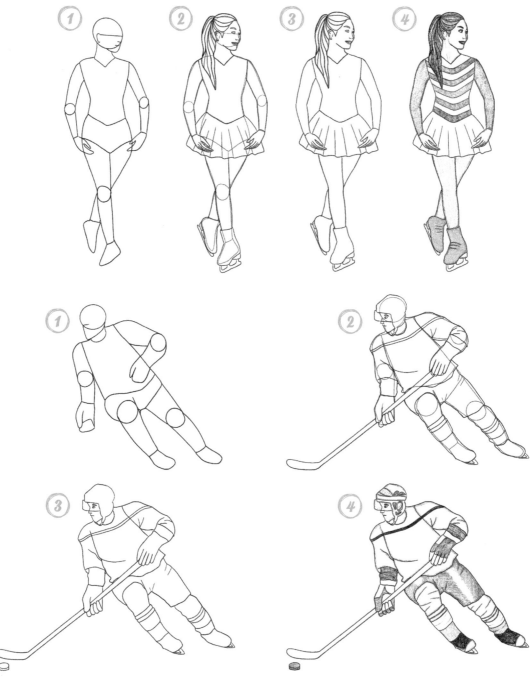

For each drawing:

1. Start with the basic body shape.

2. Add details.

3. Erase the guidelines.

4. Shade with pencil and add more details.

FASHIONABLE FRIENDS

If you like clothes, you're going to enjoy drawing this trio!

1. Start by drawing the body shapes.

2. Draw more details over the guidelines.

3. Erase the guidelines and neaten.

4. Add and define details and add shading.

DRAW BODIES A DIFFERENT WAY

You can use the head as a measurement. A general rule is: female height = seven heads; male height = eight heads. Also, two heads, one on each side of the second head from the top, makes the width. Try it and see!

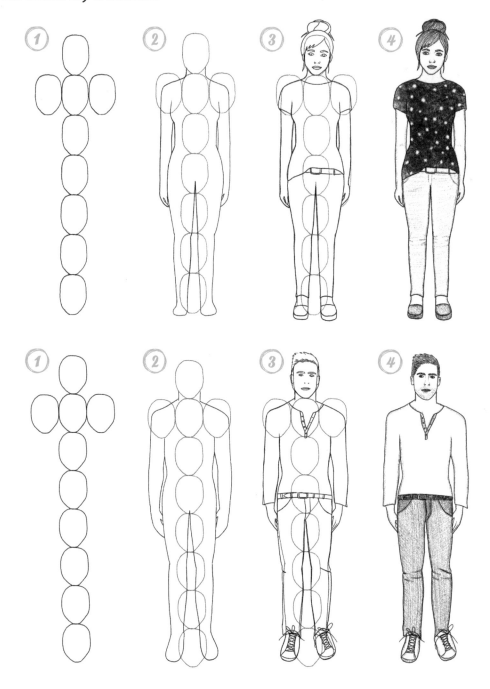

1. Draw the heads.

2. Draw the body outline.

3. Add details.

4. Erase the guidelines and add shading.

GRANDPARENTS

Here, Grandma is knitting and Grandpa is reading the newspaper.
There's a squishy couch and a bowl of cookies, too.

1. Draw the basic body shapes. Make sure the knees are bent.

2. Add details.

3. Erase the guidelines and add more details and shading.

21

FASHION DESIGNER
Clothes

BASIC PRINCIPLES FOR DRAWING CLOTHES

Even if you're not particularly interested in fashion, knowing how to draw clothes and textures comes in handy when you're drawing human characters. Clothes also play an important part in suggesting personality in an imagined character. When drawing clothes, it's important to consider the following:

A. Fabric is not perfectly straight: It can be creased, with folds and knots, depending on its position.

B. Always consider the person's figure: The fabric will form that shape. Females usually have a curved waistline compared to males.

C. Get a 3D effect: Clothing looks 3D on paper when you add folds under the fabric, too.

D. There are many ways to design a piece of clothing: You can add layers, play with cuts, and create variations.

Adding textures and patterns on clothing can dramatically alter the look. Here are examples of different patterns on one type of shirt:

JEANS

Women's jeans highlight curves and are more rounded at the waist.
Men's jeans are straighter and streamlined.

For each drawing:

1. Start with the basic outline.

2. Add details.

3. Define the features and shade lightly.

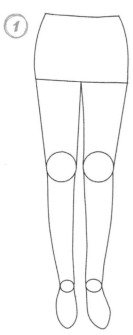
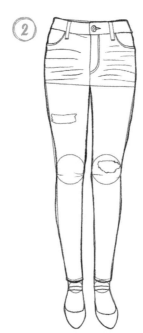
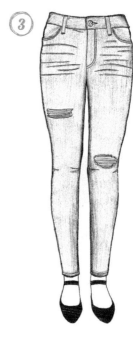

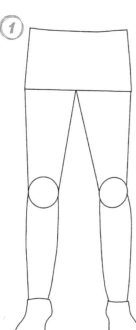
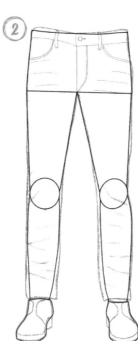

A GUIDE TO GIRLS' CLOTHING

Girls have many options when it comes to clothing. You can change patterns and styles on all of it.

Basic Formula for Shirts

A girl's shirt has a curve at the waist and a bust, while a boy's shirt is flatter. You can change the basic shirt formula to get more types of shirts by adding collars, changing sleeve length, drawing straps, adding pockets, etc.

Add variation: collars, straps

Basic Formula for Skirts

Vary the formula to draw shorts

More Outfits You Can Design:

A  B  C  D  E  F

A. Flared mini dress

B. Matching crop top and shorts

C. Off-the-shoulder top and baggy trousers

D. Peplum dress

E. Patterned maxi dress

F. Overalls

G. Long-sleeved shirt and skirt

H. Hooded jacket and pants

G  H

A GUIDE TO BOYS' CLOTHING

Clothing for boys (or men) is a lot simpler than it is for girls (or women). But you can still add a lot of variation to make interesting outfits.

Basic Formula for Shirts

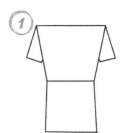   

Add variations

Basic Formula for Pants and Shorts

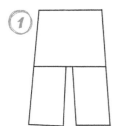   

Extras

More Outfits You Can Design:

   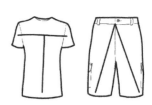

Business formal   Casual   Sporty

ARTIST TIP
A shirt has a T-shape, and pants have an upside-down V-shape.

DRAW A BALL GOWN

Ball gowns offer a lot of versatility in terms of design, fabric, shape, and decoration.

1. Start with a basic shape.

2. Add the wearer's head and hands and define the dress shape.

3. Add more details.

4. Add flower doodles on alternating folds for a graceful feel.

ARTIST TIP
Use these flower components to build your own flower patterns.

BE A SUPERHERO

Comic Books

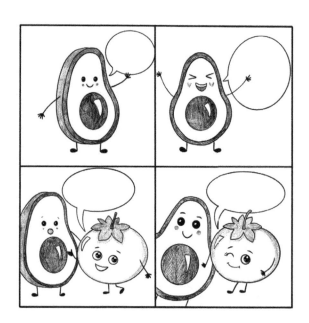

BASIC PRINCIPLES FOR DRAWING COMICS

Comics are a great way to depict a story; you can use plenty of drawing elements and as much text as needed. Unlike reading a book, comics provide you a visual concept directly. You can create a comic based on a simple idea and extend it to turn it into a graphic novel as well. The possibilities are endless. Let's go over some basic comic formats for you to start drawing.

One-Panel Comic

This is a basic comic in one square. It is usually accompanied by a title to indicate the topic. A one-panel comic emphasizes a concept, not a storyline.

In this example, you can see the main differences between a dog and cat. The cat is hopeful and independent as opposed to the dog who, judging by his expression, clearly needs a lot of love.

Are you a dog person or a cat person?

Two-Panel Comic

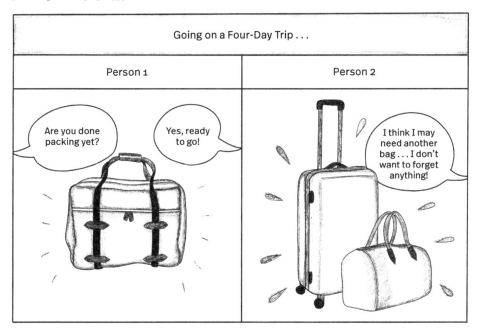

This is an extended version of the one-panel comic. Again, it focuses on a concept rather than a storyline. Two boxes are helpful for adding more details, contrast, and fun.

In this example, you can see how people's personalities affect their packing habits. Which one are you?

LONGER COMICS

After you try creating simple comics in one panel and two panels, you can move on to the next step: three-panel and four-panel comics that work on a storyline. Here are some examples:

Why I Can Never Finish a Book

This comic has a simple title to accompany it and illustrates just why the reader never seems to finish a book. First, the focus is on her environment. She's reading in bed and on the first chapter. Ten minutes later, she's fast asleep. This has probably happened to you, too!

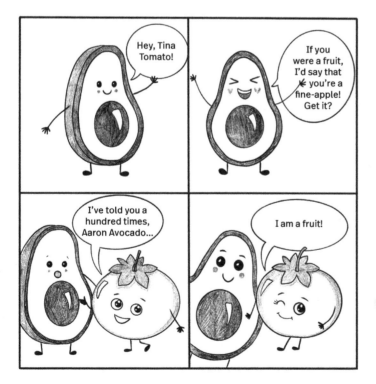

This example also shows that you have full creative license; you can depict inanimate objects as living and you can even give them names.

ARTIST TIP You can make speech bubbles in any shape. You can also write the text and then draw the bubble around it.

What I Want to Be When I Grow Up

Try drawing a three-panel comic to get your mind thinking of more ideas. This comic uses both titles and speech bubbles to make a point.

①

②

③

1. Draw a rectangle and divide it into three parts. Start by drawing the basic outlines as shown.

2. Add more details around the outlines and add a line for small titles.

3. Define with more details and shading. You can add small scenes behind the characters if you wish.

PRACTICE: A DAY AT THE BEACH

This simple comic illustrates one of the joys of spending time at the beach: finding seashells! Once you get started by finding one, it's hard to stop. Draw a square and divide it into four smaller squares. Fill them up with the following:

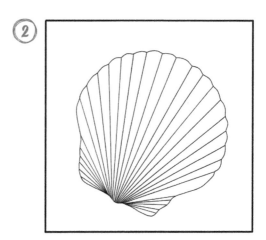

1. **Box 1:** Introduce the character. She sees something shining in the sand. Add the scenery to show where she is.

2. **Box 2:** Narrow down to what the unknown object is. Use detail to show the beauty of what she has found; seashells are pretty and interesting.

3. **Box 3:** She's getting a closer look at her discovery and marveling at it. Add a grand statement to make the point.

4. **Box 4:** One isn't enough! She finds more and more, and each one seems just as pretty as the first. Collecting seashells makes you appreciate nature even more.

Nature is a great subject when it comes to creating a comic. If you want to make a similar comic appreciating nature's beauty, try these things:

Think of an experience you had on a hike or vacation, or even in your own backyard. You might recall something that stands out.

Once you have the memory in place, think of a concept or storyline. The trick is to divide the story into action sentences; in a four-panel comic, you need four sentences. For example, in this comic they are:

1. Girl goes to beach. Something catches her eye.

2. Show close-up of what it is: a pretty seashell.

3. She adores it and can't believe she found it.

4. She builds a collection of shells and discovers that each one is beautiful in its own way.

PRACTICE: GOOD HAIR DAY

Here's another example of a four-panel box cartoon. Start by drawing a square and divide it into four boxes. The tutorial takes you step by step on filling in each box and the concept behind each illustration.

1. **Box 1:** Introduce the characters. Keep them as simple and distinct as possible so it's easy to draw again. Add possible speech bubbles.

2. **Box 2:** Draw a similar scene, except for some slight changes in their expressions; their eyebrows are slightly raised, and they are smiling to show conversation.

3. **Box 3:** Now the focus shifts to the girl and what she's thinking. Again, it's a similar drawing, but it's a close-up and her expression is slightly changed.

4. **Box 4:** This is the main part: a closer close-up to emphasize the point. You can see a major change in her face: a big smile and a wink to accentuate the point she's making.

Here is the finished cartoon! After the drawing is done, add text in the speech bubbles where there's space and use shading to make the details stand out. For the environment, a wooden table with some books and a pen have been added. Clothing is kept simple so it can be redrawn easily. Since cartoons have exaggerated facial expressions, the last box is the most important one in the story. The girl's "wink" can be further emphasized with text and some dashes and sparkles to indicate movement. Also, when you see the close-up, you can see how disheveled her hair is—despite the fact that it looks "nice" at first glance.

You can create similar cartoons focusing on one character and his or her thought or response to another.

GET CREATIVE

Animals

BASIC PRINCIPLES FOR DESIGNED ANIMALS

You can come up with innovative designs using animals and other elements. Here are some combinations to get your creative mind going:

Shape of animal + element = silhouette style

Animal torso + banner = portrait focus

Animal + wreath = decorative style

Animal + flower elements = quirky cartoon style

You can also create designs using human and animal elements. This creates a fantasy-inspired effect. For example, this girl can be transformed with a **koi fish theme** or a flower antler crown.

GEOMETRIC ANIMALS

Geometric structures are a fun way to draw animals. You can practice drawing lines and create a unique design every time.

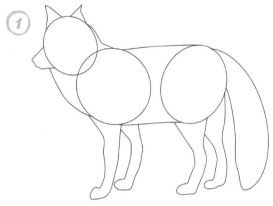

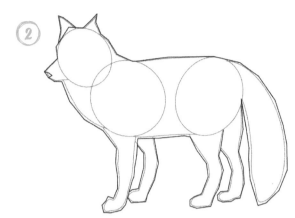

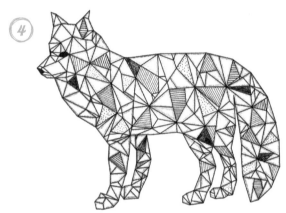

1. Draw the basic shapes.

2. Draw around the outline with small, straight lines.

3. Add adjoining shapes. They can be triangles, quadrilaterals, etc. Start at one corner and fill the body.

4. Add more lines within these shapes to make a dense design. You can fill these shapes with these textures:

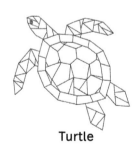

Turtle

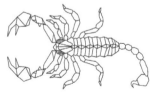

Scorpion

Bear   Hummingbird

ANIMAL ELEMENTS

Combine an animal with another element to create a cute result. You can use these animals as wall art, on party invitations, or on graduation and other announcements.
    For each drawing:

1. Draw the basic shapes.

2. Add details.

3. Erase the guidelines and shade lightly to define details.

Llama and cactus: Great for party invitations.

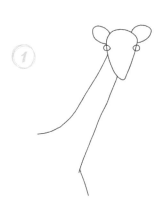  

Giraffe with floral crown: Perfect for greeting cards, wall art, and baby announcements.

Owl with glasses and graduation cap: Fun for your own graduation or for a friend.

MANDALA STAG SILHOUETTE

If you like doodling, try adding mandala details in an animal silhouette. You can draw them with any animal silhouette: Here's a stag.

1. Draw a basic outline; include antlers for a more spectacular effect.

2. Draw wavy lines for the antlers and draw a mandala design in different parts. To draw a mandala, draw a dot or a small circle and add details around it so it gets bigger.

3. Keep adding more details and layers in the mandala.

4. Add finer details within the sections of the mandala and shade lightly.

HALF GIRL, HALF LION

You can use this theme with other variations: half boy, half wolf, etc. This is a good rainy-day project when you feel too lazy to draw one thing properly—why not try drawing two halves?

1. Draw a vertical line and add basic guidelines.

2. Add more details.

3. Define the earlier lines with pencil strokes.

4. Add volume by shading.

24

Watercolor Fun

BASIC PRINCIPLES OF WATERCOLORS

One thing that makes a black-and-white drawing stand out is a pop of color! Here are the basics of watercolor.

First, collect your supplies: watercolors (any brand will do), paintbrushes, some thick paper, and a cup filled with water. You can buy watercolor paper, but if you don't have that, any sturdy paper is fine.

Next, make some swatches with the colors you have. Color swatches are helpful because you can see how the colors look on paper as opposed to guessing what they look like from the paint packaging.

You can transform your pencil sketches with watercolor. Just remember to draw as lightly as possible with pencil to keep the focus on the colors.

Watercolor works with . . . water. So, add water to activate your paints. You can blend colors together when the paints are wet. Paint one color, and before it dries, paint another color next to it. They will blend together. Remember, watercolor doesn't have to be perfect to be beautiful. Imperfection in the tones adds to its beauty.

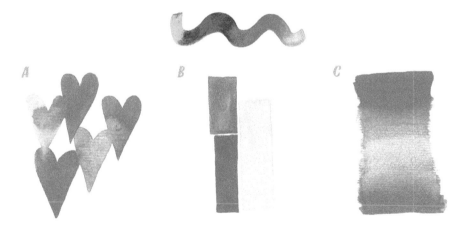

A. **Watercolor bleeds:** One color bleeds into another.

B. **Solid tones:** Use one color to fill in a shape.

C. **Gradients:** Add paint on one side and then change the values with more or less water.

WATERCOLOR SHAPES

A

Free-form shapes are great for practicing watercolor. In this exercise, you explore how water and paint interact to create art that is different every time.

A. **Circles:** Start by painting a circle, and while the paint is still wet, paint another circle touching it. You'll notice the color "bleeds" from one circle to the other, making blended colors. Keep filling up the page with circles—some small, some big.

B

B. **Triangles:** Paint a triangle and then an adjacent triangle before it dries. Vary the triangle sizes to get an interesting pattern.

C. **Rectangles:** Paint rectangles placed in both horizontal and vertical directions and watch the colors merge.

C

WATERCOLOR LEAVES

Leaves are great fun to paint with watercolor. You can change colors and shapes, create clusters, and more. Draw the leafy shape with pencil lightly and then paint over it.

Basic Formula for Freehand Leaves

Here are two examples of leaves with different structures:

1. Lightly draw an outline in pencil.

2. Paint over the pencil outline with the tip of your paintbrush.

3. Before the outline dries completely, fill it in with color.

4. Let the shape dry, and then use a darker shade to add veins. Any outline that still shows can be erased if you like.

A. **Multicolored leaf cluster:** Remember, watercolor looks better when it has a dreamy, imperfect feel. Be as messy as you wish. It will still look good.

Start by lightly drawing a curved line.

Work on each leaf separately: Use different colors and watch them blend.

B. **Different leaf shapes:** The great thing about leaves is that you can totally make them up.

Draw different leaf shapes, then color them with paint.

You can make leaves with rounded or pointy edges, combine small leaves with larger ones, mix colors, etc.

C. **Leafy wreaths:** Use a repeating leaf pattern to create a wreath, or add different kinds of leaves to jazz it up.

FLOWER GARDEN

These five-petal flowers are great for practicing watercolor. You can use this simple design to make cards, as embellishments on project covers, and more.

Basic Formula for Flowers

Here you can lightly pencil in the details and fill with paint.

Extras: buds and leaves

1. Draw a light pencil outline.

2. Paint over the pencil outline with the tip of your paintbrush.

3. Before the outline dries completely, fill it in with color.

4. Let it dry and then add a circle inside.

1. Paint flowers and buds of different colors and sizes.

2. Let dry and then add stems, leaves, and circles on the flowers.

You can make the designs as crowded or as simple as you want.

NEGATIVE PAINTING TECHNIQUE

Negative painting is when you add color around an object instead of filling it in. You can use different layers as well. It sounds complicated but is really quite simple.

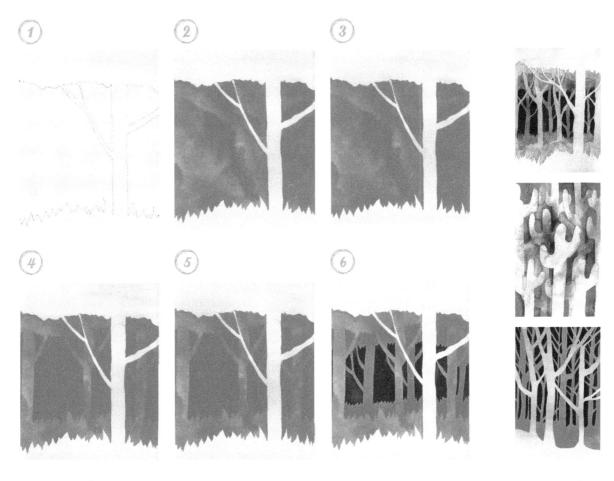

1. Start by painting your paper a light color. Draw a tree with grass.
2. Paint around the tree and grass with a darker color (e.g., orange).
3. Lightly draw the next layer of trees in the background with pencil.
4. Paint around these trees with an even darker color (e.g., red).
5. Lightly draw another set of trees on the red layer with pencil.
6. Paint around these trees with black.

ARTIST TIP
Try thin, tall branches; a forest in green; or cactus layers.

Index

Acknowledgments

This book is made possible by the wonderful folks at Callisto Media. A special thanks to Vanessa Putt for getting me on board, Katie Moore for her helpful feedback, William Mack for his guidance and creative direction, Vanessa Ta for her thorough editing, Lisa Dusenbery and Erum Khan (to name just a few people) for their proofreading, and the rest of the team for making this an awesome learning experience. I'm so grateful to them for giving me the opportunity to share what I know!

I also would like to thank my friends and family: especially my sisters Diya and Drishti, my parents Alka and Sandeep, and grandparents Bimal and Shobha who supported me throughout writing and illustrating this book. They also may have wanted to get their names mentioned ☺.

And of course, I would like to offer thanks to more than a million people who check their phones every day to see what I'm drawing and painting on social media. This book is dedicated to all of you. Stay creative!

—Aaria

About the Author

Aaria Baid is an artist, blogger, and writer. She documents her daily art adventures at @surelysimpleblog on Instagram, which is at a million followers and growing with like-minded people who like art for the sake of making art. She is a multitasker and also hosts (and curates) creative art and calligraphy challenges on her various projects: @surelysimplechallenge, @surelysimplewords, @opinion9, and @patternvilla. Visit her websites: SurelySimple.com and Opinion9.com to get insights into her creative process. She loves art and calligraphy, experimenting with (and collecting) stationery and art supplies, connecting with people, and keeping life surely simple.

CPSIA information can be obtained
at www.ICGtesting.com
Printed in the USA
JSHW052147150821
17812JS00006B/7